THE U...

...INC...

BASICS

A BEGINNER'S GUIDE TO STAGE SOUND

Peter Coleman

**ENTERTAINMENT
TECHNOLOGY PRESS**

Educational Series

Illustrations by Jackie Staines

BASICS
A BEGINNER'S GUIDE TO STAGE SOUND

Peter Coleman

Entertainment Technology Press

Basics
A Beginner's Guide to Stage Sound

© Peter Coleman

First edition Published July 2004 by
Entertainment Technology Press Ltd
The Studio, High Green, Great Shelford, Cabridge CB2 5EG
Internet: www.etnow.com

ISBN 1 904031 27 7

A title within the
Entertainment Technology Press Educational Series
Series editor: John Offord

CODE / SBAS001

CONTENTS

ACKNOWLEDGEMENTS

With thanks to:

Jo Beaumont-Ward
Steve Chappell
Saul Eagles

And all at Stage Electrics who have given me encouragement and support.

INTRODUCTION

For those of you who have read *Basics – A Beginner's Guide to Stage Lighting*, and were perhaps surprised at how it strayed from the title, you probably won't be too surprised that this book is going to do the same.

If you haven't experienced the book, let me try to sum it up simply: if you thought that the lighting side of the performing arts was complex and difficult, just wait until you start on performance sound!

Some would say, with a fair degree of justification, that this whole topic of Performance Sound is far too complex to be covered in any form of *basic* format, and that a little information is a dangerous thing; as such this book is likely to give only snapshot information and not the full and detailed level of understanding needed. I can't disagree with that argument, except for one cast iron fact.

There are many, probably thousands of people, spread across the UK who will never get anywhere near what may rudely be called 'a proper job' when putting together a performance sound system. In my view there are two main reasons why this is the case: firstly, lack of information, and secondly, lack of budget.

Let me say straightaway that I am not a trained or qualified acoustic engineer, but then I don't expect you are either. So why am I being silly enough to attempt to compile an explanation of what can be a very exacting science? The answer is in the title. It's the *Basics* of the job and hopefully, some simple explanations to some of the mysteries and, along the way, some of the pitfalls that I will be trying to help you with.

During my time working in live theatre and the performing arts, I have seen many changes in what has become the accepted level of performance sound equipment or, more correctly, the performance output of the equipment involved.

I remember that in the first theatre I worked in, The Grand in Wolverhampton, the amplifiers – there were two – were valve amps with EL34 valves and the great upgrade of the day was when they got changed to new units using KT88s. All this will mean very little to many of you, except to question my age, but the point is that in this fast moving technological age, we are now using products that would be totally unrecognisable to users of those old valve amplifiers, except of course for the undoubted improvement in quality and capacity of the end product.

This is not intended to be a walk down my personal memory lane, but alongside those valve amplifiers, there were column loudspeakers, with multiple 6′x4′ elliptical speakers and the sound mixer was an upright panel in the prompt corner fitted with rotary pots, *not the modern linear fader strips,* and only a global 'tone' control, all of course a million miles away from what we use today.

I will try not to get too technical, but I fear that with this very technical discipline, there are bound to be a few things that may at first seem rather complex. Bear with me and believe me, if I can come to terms with it, then so can you, and at least you may then have a better appreciation of what performance sound is all about in your venue.

Here I should qualify the nature of the term 'venue' and just what type of venue this book and my experience is all about. It's not aimed at outdoor or even large venue users; neither is it referenced to the broadcast or recording venue or the music industry. So what's left? Theatre and Performing Arts venues – most everything from the school or village hall to the 1000-seat theatre auditorium.

As with my previous *Basics* publication I offer the following plea for your understanding. It's not a 'story', nor is it a real 'reference work'. It's not intended to be the complete and finished article giving specific answers to all your questions. It's just a few *Basics* that I hope you will find helpful.

I think I should qualify it all with at least two alternative titles: '*Some information on how to assemble a performance sound system*' or '*This may not solve all your problems*'.

PROLOGUE

I believe it's vitally important to cover sound amplification, the most important element in the equation, at the outset. You want to use, or believe you have a need to use, sound amplification equipment in your venue. Are you sure? It might seem a rather silly question to ask, but how do you know?

There are two questions for starters and they are probably quite simple to answer. Or are they?

1. Are you using sound equipment because your group or the venue has always used it? Obviously if you need sound for effect, the car arriving, an aeroplane flying over, etc, then that's understandable. However, if you are planning to amplify the spoken or singing voice, are you sure that you need to do so?

2. Have you considered the acoustic properties of your venue? What is the natural room (for room read hall or auditorium, etc) acoustic like? Is it a good hearing room? You might be working in a 1200 seat Victorian auditorium, where because of the shape and construction materials used, the spoken word, in a normal voice, can be clearly heard at every seat. You may be working in a modern building, with only three or four hundred seats, where because of the shape and building materials, the same voice can hardly be heard anywhere!

Of course we are all now applying today's standards in our work, otherwise we would all still be driving around in model T Fords, but just sometimes the rush to use all the modern technical aids can make us miss the obvious best way forward, and a judgement as to whether or not to use some form of amplification may not rest entirely with you.

Obviously there are some forms of performance, and some venues, where we all quite naturally accept the unaided acoustic end product. I just ask you to pause and to consider the 20th century advent of amplified sound as being the norm for every occasion. Try to think when and where you last experienced a wholly acoustic performance. Could you hear the intended end product?

I'm not trying to make a case for more acoustic and less amplified works – and in any case there may well be very good and justified reasons why amplification should be used.

You will often find that once you start with the amplification of sound within your venue, it will snowball out of control in a quite alarming manner. I cite two cases as evidence of my point, these being actual case histories, not tall stories.

1. A medium-sized hall with less than 500 seats (somewhere in the Midlands) has a group of users who, with all the best intent, have developed the level of sound used in the hall, to the extent that the forestage/orchestra pit area now has 30+ microphone tie lines permanently installed to the sound mixer position, in order to amplify the orchestra. The result of all this is that just to get over the level of sound created by the orchestra, every principal performer on stage has to use a radio microphone and all of the chorus work needs microphones. Now I'm not sure which came first, the microphones picking up the performers on stage, or those picking up the musicians in the orchestra, but I can take a guess, although it matters very little. What matters is the end product, and I'm sure the paying customers think it's just fine, even if the level of sound created is enough to shake the windows of the shops across the road in the street outside, never mind the actual hall itself. No I'm not saying it's wrong, it obviously works for that group and its regular audiences, and as most of their works are of the musical style, rather than straight plays or poetry readings, it's the style and the norm that is accepted.

2. Back in the early 1970s I was working at the Hippodrome Theatre in Birmingham when Morecambe & Wise came for two nights, a Friday and Saturday, with two shows each night at 6.15 and 8.30 (performance times you don't see very often today) and of course they sold out, including the standing room, which meant that the audience was just over 2000. Friday's shows were fine and so was the first house on Saturday – then disaster struck! While the second house was filling up, the main rack containing all of the amplifiers literally blew up! A flash, a big bang, and a lot of smoke. Oh dear, no sound system! And with just 10 minutes to curtain up and most people in their seats, it wasn't a problem that was easy to resolve. Coming from a background of 'Music Hall' where they had spent years learning their trade, the two stars took it all in their stride. Never was there a thought of delaying or cancelling the show, they just got on with it. One of the musicians in the band gave up his guitar amplifier, which was placed directly in front of the centre stage microphone, and with this somewhat mis-matched microphone and very small single amplifier, they simply went out and did the show.

The amplification was minimal, the audience loved it, and no one complained they couldn't hear. No one demanded their money back. I rest my case.

There is one other factor, which is vital to the success of a group of people – we'll call them the audience – hearing an acoustic output from an instrument or voice and that is the clarity and volume of that output.

We all appreciate that an instrument or a human voice can be made to sound soft and gentle, or loud and even very loud, and I think most would accept that, in our normal daily activities, if we find that we need to make ourselves heard to a large room full of people, even just 20 or 30, then we will probably raise our voice. Why do we do that? Obviously it's a natural thing to do. We know that if we don't, then those furthest away may not hear what we are saying.

In these 'modern' times we have all come to rely on the wonders of the technological age to give us help in what we do – the sound system amplification equipment in a performance space being just one such example. I know it sounds 'very old', but sadly almost everyone now expects that the sound system will enable him or her to 'perform' in a natural voice, but of course this will be delivered, with total clarity, to every seat in the auditorium.

So with this modern day mindset and almost total reliance on the technical, rather than an individual's ability to project the voice, I fear that the days of the acoustic, spoken vocal performance are now coming to an end.

So where does this leave us in the consideration of an acoustic or an amplified performance choice? No further forward really, and since this book is about the use and application of sound equipment, I had better stop ducking the issue and start giving you some information.

1 THE ACOUSTICS OF THE ROOM

When I said I was going to give you some information, I hope you didn't think I was going to tell you what equipment to use and where and how to use it? I hope not, because you might just be about to ask for your money back! Yes, I will get around to 'the equipment' eventually, but not just yet. Before we go hanging loudspeakers all over the place and using sound mixing desks, there are one or two rather serious things we need to consider.

Now that I have got the acoustic versus amplified requirement out of my system, the next most important factor is the room acoustic you are going to be working with? This will vary immensely, from the massively reverberant to the almost totally dead flat.

I should try to explain those two terms: *reverberant* and *flat*.

Reverberant (often called 'live'), as you would guess from the name, is where the sound generated in the space has an almost echo-like property. Echo is different and should not be confused with reverberation – as the sound waves generated bounce around the room.

Flat (often called 'dead'), is simply the opposite of reverberant, where the sound generated does not reverberate. Generally, all outdoor locations are regarded as flat, but don't run away with the idea that sound in the great outdoors does not sometimes suffer from some form of reverberation.

Most rooms will be reverberant to some degree; it's just a matter of how much they reverberate, which will make them friendly or not to your ears and thus your hearing ability. By the way, in order for your ear to give your brain an acceptable sound, it needs to contain some level of reflected sound or reverberance.

I'm not going to delve too deeply into the science of acoustics and how the human ear works, much less the design considerations of a performance space. Let's face it, you aren't likely to be building your own auditorium, or if you were, you would be basing your building requirements on someone far better qualified than me to help you. The situation almost all of us find ourselves in, is that we are put to work in a place and acoustic surrounding not of our choice or design, so we have to make the best of what we've got.

I have to labour the point here, that although the array of modern equipment is both powerful and comprehensive, you still can't go out and buy a little black box that will make it all come right as if by magic, although we are getting close.

It is still the case that if you have a room with a poor acoustic that needs treating, then it's not the equipment that you look to first, it's the mechanical changes to the room that will help you most.

We have to start somewhere, so let's take a look at what will be probably the most used type of space in the country: the ubiquitous school hall. I'm not criticising school halls or even the people who design them, but generally they are dreadful places on all fronts and often the acoustics are the worst aspect of all. Just consider why. It's got everything to do with their multi-use requirements: a big open hall space to get several hundred pupils into for an assembly, probably a dining hall at lunch time, maybe a gymnasium or sports court during the day and, oh yes, somebody stuck a stage at one end so it must also be the school theatre! It doesn't matter if it was built in 1952 or 2002 – the build parameters and criteria are still much the same.

More often than not, what you end up with is the standard rectangular six sided box and by the nature of the design, which had absolutely no acoustic consideration, probably five of those six sides are built, or at least finished in some sort of hard reflective surface – reflective to sound that is.

The result is a room with a 'very lively reflective characteristic' and that's a very mild description of what they actually sound like, which is best made using words that my publisher will only delete so I won't bother using!

I know of one such new-build multi-purpose hall, where the reverberant acoustic was so bad that the P.E. teacher, unable to make herself heard, over the clatter of 30 pairs of feet on the hardwood floor, had to use a whistle to bring the students to a standstill, so that an instruction could be given and heard by the class. You can perhaps imagine what it must have sounded like with a few instruments and a chorus of voices?

This brings me to the nub of the hearing issue in all performance spaces, the *intelligibility level.* In other words, is what you are hearing understandable? Can you actually hear and disseminate one word or sound from the last or the next? It's this factor that makes a good hearing acoustic; if your room has it, rejoice. If it doesn't, then all is not lost, but as I said, don't think that your sound system equipment is going to solve your problem; it almost certainly won't.

As I said, thinking about the five sides of the rectangle of the hall (the sixth side is probably the stage, so it will probably have curtains, scenery, even people on it, so its reflective properties are reduced), each surface will probably be a hard reflective surface. The floor will be wooden or a hard sports mat type surface, the ceiling could be a decorative wood finish or at best a lay-in grid tile ceiling, with quite a low sound absorption rate, the walls may be block or brick finish and one or both side walls could have floor to ceiling glazing, everything reflecting sound off itself. If that is that not bad enough, all the surfaces will be built in nice straight lines with right angles. The sound simply bounces off one surface, hits the surface directly opposite and comes straight back. By the way, if the hall had a regular curve or barrel-shaped ceiling that would probably be even more of a reflective problem. At its worst, if you stand in the middle of the hall and clap your hands, the resultant reverberation sounds like a round of applause. At best, you will hear the clap repeated several times, finally dying away.

Where you put a sound source, amplified or acoustic, into this type of space

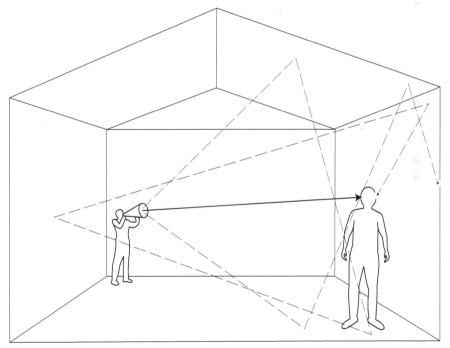

The listener receives a mixture of direct ('flat') sound straight from the megaphone, and reverberated ('live') sound that has bounced around the hard surfaces of the room.

you start off with what may be classified as *direct sound*. In practice, unless you are inside a totally controlled non-reflective room, true direct sounds don't really exist, because you will also be hearing *reflections* of the same sound that started out as a direct sound. The reflections can be roughly categorised into two types: early and late, or short and long. The early reflections are, if you like, good for you. They are what make the sound you hear have a depth. Some would describe it as a colour, but the late reflections are not so good and there comes a point when these can downgrade the sound you hear, because it becomes too reverberant. I hope you are still with me after all this. I fear that I'm going a little too far, but I did say it was an exacting science and believe me, I'm only scratching the surface. But it's enough for you to know that there is a fine balance to be had in making your hall produce the right level of reverberation.

Try a simple experiment in your performance hall and either with a stopwatch or just your own count, see how long the reverberation lasts. If you get down to around one second that's quite good, 1.5 to 2.5 is about the average, above 2.5 and you are going to have to think about taking some course of action. Remember that new multi-use hall I mentioned? It measured at almost seven seconds! If you have one of those, don't phone me. You could, of course, invite the architect, the consulting engineer, and if it ever had one, the acoustician, to the first night performance, and ask them to stand up and explain themselves to the audience.

In truth, if you have a real problem space, with this level of reverberance, you have to take some serious action. The one surface you may not be able to change is the floor, but to some degree this will take care of itself. Assuming that your audience is seated, it and the seating will go a long way to break up the reflective nature of the floor. Incidentally this is one reason why almost all performance venues will notice a change to their acoustic properties, depending on the size of the audience. Of course, if you were able to lay matting or carpet on your reflective floor, then that would be the best plan.

The ceiling may also present a problem, not least in terms of access, and once you have got up to it, what can you hope to achieve? It's difficult because firstly it's likely to be the main source of lighting in the hall, and secondly the performance lighting equipment may well be hanging from it, so it may not be possible to do much with it.

The three walls – two sides and one end – remember the stage forms the other wall, are what you can probably do most with. Curtains, (many), or at least soft fabric wall covering panels, will reduce the reflective property of the hard surface of walls or glazing.

Something I will guarantee is that the mechanical treatment and changing of your hall acoustic will be neither simple, nor cheap, nor a total cure to your problem. My usual comment is that very few things you do to try to treat the acoustic problem will by themselves provide a cure. It is more likely that the combination of the changes you make will add up to a noticeable improvement.

Of course the very best solution to all this would have been to have the hall designed and constructed with its acoustic properties high on the priority list. Sadly, unless the original build project was driven by someone who championed the acoustic requirement and it had a sizeable budget, this is not likely to have happened. It's worth noting that even when places do get built with the time and money spent with the acoustics in mind, it doesn't always work out quite as intended. I know of places where I and many other users would say that this is the case.

A final note on the acoustics of a space are the reverberation and hearing properties. Yes, it's the reflective nature of the hall that may give a problem and this is compounded, even, excuse the use of the word 'amplified', by the angles of the opposing surfaces and the distances between them. This is 'an exacting science', and so it is perhaps even more difficult when you are trying to make changes to an existing space. Many of the things I am talking about are quite variable, and affect and interact with each other. Consider the reverberation factor and my statements about hard reflective surfaces. How is it, then, that the inside of an enclosed telephone box, with all its hard reflective surfaces, is not reverberant? Indeed it's quite the opposite, having quite a flat acoustic. That's because of the distances involved or, in the case of the telephone box, the lack of distance.

So, all of these factors will affect how you hear what you hear, and the *what* part will determine the level of intelligibility.

When you stop to think about the natural acoustic properties of your space, particularly your school hall, and the shape and building materials used, try to compare it with somewhere else you know, maybe a theatre auditorium that has a better natural acoustic. I expect you will find, that in the purpose-built auditorium, the floor will be covered with carpet and have fixed fabric covered seats, that the walls may be decorated with some sort of fabric finish and that the ceiling contains a decorative pattern. The floor and seating may be raked, the walls, indeed the shape of the auditorium, may not just be a simple rectangle or square. The better auditorium has gone some way to remove or change the building shape and those reflective surfaces. Now at least you can start to understand some of the problems involved in making your space deliver a good quality of sound.

2 STARTING AT THE END

A little like your personal tastes in the choice of colour for a lighting design, each of us will have our own likes and dislikes in what we hear. Now we may not be able to do much about the content, but if it's your job to sort out the sound, then everyone will expect you to deliver their own personal choice. Not so easy.

When dealing with lighting in *Basics – A Beginner's Guide to Stage Lighting*, I made the point about people being colour-blind, and everyone not seeing exactly what you may see. Well, there is something similar with sound: our individual capacity to hear things or, more correctly, not to hear things.

In people with normal hearing at birth and in our early years of life, our hearing ability is at its most acute, other reference books will give you more precise information, should you need it, but at this age we can hear sounds and frequencies from as low as 50Hz right up to 18kHz (50 to 18,000). As we get older, our ability to hear things at each end of the hearing spectrum will diminish. Of course everyone will be affected in a slightly different way, and we all have relatives who exhibit this, even if only to prove how wide the variation is. My mother, who lived to be nearly ninety, could hear a pin drop in the next room, in her later years, my father, on the other hand, had to wear a hearing aid in his later life.

It is generally accepted that as we age, we will probably lose several hundred Hertz capacity at the lower end and several thousand Hertz from the upper end of our hearing ability scale. So, before we do anything with sound we must appreciate that we have to cater for an audience that has a different hearing capacity.

Sorry I've gone technical on you. Let me try to explain. The spectrum of hearing is described and measured in two ways: firstly, the frequency of the sound, first calculated by Heinrich Hertz (1857 – 94). The Hertz is a unit of frequency in the SI (Systém international d'unités) system being equal to one cycle per second. Then secondly, by its volume, calculated by the Bel (after Alexander Graham Bell) – a unit used for comparing two levels of power (in this case sound) intensity equal to the logarithm to the base 10 of the ratio of the two levels, hence the *Deci*-bel. Hertz is abbreviated to Hz and Bel converted to Decibel and thus dB.

Part of my working day is now spent making specifications for all aspects of technical equipment used in the performing arts – performance sound being just one element of it. I have stock phrases that I use at the very first opportunity when meeting with a new client to discuss their requirements. I used one right at the start of this book: if you thought that the lighting side of the performing arts was complex and difficult, just wait until you start on the performance sound!

But the one I want to concentrate on now gets us a little closer to the real start of the equipment trail. Sound system equipment, being an assembly of many parts linking together, is only as good as its weakest link.

I usually qualify this by saying that you can spend thousands of pounds on loudspeakers, amplifiers and mixers, but if you have gone out to a high street shop and bought a low-price microphone, then the whole system is likely to sound only as good as the cost of the microphone – not the loudspeakers and all the other expensive things. In short, in sound system assembly you get what you pay for.

One rather strange fact about any sound system is that it's almost certain the equipment involved will be drawn from more than just one manufacturer. You will find major brand name manufacturers for individual component parts, but none of them can provide the complete package, although a couple would give you an argument about it, mainly in the small, almost domestic market, but not in professional performance sound use. So you are bound to have to put a system together from a selection of parts coming from different manufacturers. This fact alone makes it very difficult for those outside the industry to assess just how the component parts will work together, and to make sure that there are no weak links in the equipment chain.

Because of this weakest link situation, it is very difficult to help those of you who already have some sort of sound system in your venue but would like to improve it. The best way forward in this situation is to let me try to explain a little more of the information and indeed the philosophy involved in putting the component parts together. Then you will have a better understanding of what you may need to do with your existing system.

From this point, let me try to lead you through some of the decision making, coupled with some of the technical information, which I believe is vital in the planning process required to put a sound system in place. We will probably dip in and out of this simple scenario as we go along.

This chapter is entitled 'starting at the end'. Well, the real end point is your ears, and one step back from that is the physical distance from your ears to the loudspeakers, which are outputting the sounds you are listening to. Now, we know we can't do anything about the hearing ability of the audience (always variable) but we can have some useful input into the distance factor between the loudspeaker and the seated audience. More of that later, but the 'end' that I'm going the start with is the choice and arrangement of the loudspeakers.

It's a little like the lighting job; lanterns (loudspeakers) in the wrong place simply can't do the job – no matter how much they cost, or how well specified the rest of the equipment is. There are several critical factors here involving the loudspeakers: the power output, the dispersion (angle of coverage) the location, and the type and suitability. The last of these may seem rather obscure. But what I'm talking about is correct in its description.

You need to consider just what it is that your loudspeakers have to provide. Is it a relatively low level of sound amplification for the spoken word such as in a lecture theatre? Is it for live music? Or even for a loud disco environment? In this choice you have the first of many decisions to make, and without some more knowledge of the topic, how can you make a choice?

Looking at the average loudspeaker box, you will probably find that it actually contains not one, but two or even three, loudspeaker devices, each outputting a specific frequency range of sound. You will see at the bottom of the box the traditional speaker shape device, called a *woofer*, which handles the low frequency sounds. Then in the centre or top of the box, you will find a smaller device called a *tweeter* or *compression driver*, which takes care of the mid and high range frequencies. Finally at the top, assuming three devices are used, you will see a *horn*. This is actually another compression driver but with a specific directional, horn-shaped output, which gives the mid and high frequencies the ability to project sounds over a greater distance at a specific angle of coverage. This packaging of multiple loudspeaker devices into one unit is more correctly described

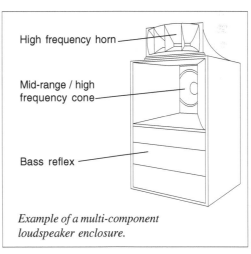

High frequency horn

Mid-range / high frequency cone

Bass reflex

Example of a multi-component loudspeaker enclosure.

as a *loudspeaker enclosure* but we all tend to call it a loudspeaker. Obviously the component parts, or loudspeaker devices, are changed and mixed to give the desired output, i.e. in a bass or sub bass loudspeaker there would only be a requirement for the woofer device, as mid and high range frequencies are not required.

Let's consider a few of the options in the types of loudspeaker available to you.

1. The Full Range Loudspeaker

As the name implies, each loudspeaker enclosure outputs sound across the complete range of hearing frequencies. So from the very low (*bass*) to the very high, they all come out of the same loudspeaker enclosure. As explained previously, this type of loudspeaker will use two or three of the device types, providing the full range coverage required, from just one loudspeaker.

2. The Sub Bass Loudspeaker

Again as the name implies, this time the loudspeaker enclosure only outputs the very low bass frequencies and none of the others.

3. The Bi-Amp Loudspeaker

In exterior appearance, it may look just like the full range box, but it relies on having two amplified signals being fed to it, one usually dedicated to the bass frequencies, the other for all of the other frequencies

4. The Tri-Amp Loudspeaker

Similar to the Bi-Amp, but requiring three different amplification feeds, bass, middle and high frequencies.

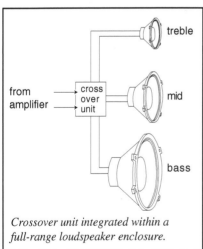

Crossover unit integrated within a full-range loudspeaker enclosure.

N.B. The full range loudspeaker will contain a device called a crossover, which effectively splits the signal from one amplifier into the various individual frequencies used by the individual loudspeaker devices.

The Bi-Amp and Tri-Amp loudspeakers require the frequencies fed individually from dedicated amplifiers, to the corresponding section of the loudspeaker.

I'm going to stop the description of loudspeaker types there, because although there are other types of loudspeaker, 100 Volt line, line array, horn-loaded, the list goes on. In general, they are rather specialist in what they do, and remember my comments here are intended to be – basic.

I'm sure that you can all see the need for a dedicated loudspeaker to cope with the bass frequency elements of sound, but what benefits do the other types bring? Well, more accuracy in the treatment of a particular frequency, not only in the amplification of the signal, but also in the changes and variation that can be made to it, only available as a global whole when using the full range loudspeaker.

It's like your choice of a motor car, we probably all start off with a saloon or hatchback, but our use dictates that some of us have an estate model or an MPV, or even a minibus or a van. You get the idea? The choice is brought down to the most commonly used requirement, so for the sake of keeping it simple, let's for the moment assume the use of the full range loudspeaker arrangement, within our simple scenario.

I must make the point here, that I'm not writing this to champion any one particular brand or make of loudspeaker. Recent years have seen a proliferation of makes and models; a little like lanterns in a lighting rig, they are all mostly black boxes and hang up in the air! Only if you have strong anorak tendencies will you be very bothered who makes it and why it's different or better than the next ten manufacturers' products, which just happen to look almost identical and have very similar technical specifications. Yes, your chosen loudspeaker will need to conform to certain standards and perform to specific performance parameters, and the one thing that may help you as you wade your way through the minefield of options on offer, is the fact that, as with so many things in life, the more you pay for it, the better it's likely to perform.

I don't disguise the fact that people like me, who make their living from specifying all sorts of technical equipment, do have our favourites. I'm fortunate that I'm not tied to a specific manufacturer, so my main criteria in the choice of equipment, in this case loudspeakers, is: a) whether it is the right specification for the venue and users' needs, and b) what is its known track record for reliability. Then would come value for money (always very difficult to quantify), ease of installation (some are more difficult than others) and aesthetics (colour options if relevant, weights and sizes). These last three considerations do change places in order of importance, but the first two, for me, are not options to change. Loudspeaker options and choices over, having settled on the full range loudspeakers for your venue, you now have some more choices to make.

I'm going to ramble off at a tangent again, so stay with me. Remember that old valve amplifier I encountered years ago? Well, I think it was rated at about 50 Watts per channel. These days you will find that sort of capacity in the hi-fi system in home use, or even the system in your car.

We have all learned that one factor in making a sound system have the level of intelligibility we desire, is to make sure that it can deliver enough sound pressure level (SPL) into the seated area, and to do this you need to have an arrangement of loudspeakers, correctly sized, to do the job.

Going back a few years, we would regularly talk about a loudspeaker in terms of its Wattage, the idea being that the more Wattage it could handle, the more sound would come out of it. That's not wholly wrong, but we are now more interested in the SPL and a few other more subtle factors.

This choice of being correctly sized is not just a matter of putting in bigger loudspeakers – size isn't everything here. Another of those vitally important factors is the signal dispersion, (the angle of coverage) from the front of the loudspeaker, where we are primarily interested in the mid and high frequencies. The bass frequencies will find their way to all parts of the auditorium, but those mid and high frequencies need to be focused in the same way that a lantern would be, as it's these frequencies that contain the vast majority of the information that we need to hear and to differentiate between different sounds. In other words, to make what we hear intelligible.

When you look into the specification for the loudspeaker, one of the things you should see is a detail for the dispersion. It will say something like: "dispersion 90° x 60°", that's 90° in the horizontal and 60° in the vertical. In looking to position a pair of loudspeakers in your traditionally shaped hall, try drawing a scale plan of the seated area, and position the loudspeakers at the proscenium position looking back into the seating, then look at the 90° angle from both loudspeakers, and see if it covers your seating, particularly at the front centre position. A note of caution here, just because the loudspeaker claims to have a 90° coverage, don't expect that the extremities of the coverage range will be as good, or perform as well as the centre of the coverage range. It almost certainly won't, and how much this varies can be seen on a performance graph of the loudspeakers performance. The budget conscious loudspeaker (I didn't really want to use the word cheaper) may not have this information readily available. If not, beware. The more expensive product, on the other hand, will proudly boast reams of data to support claims of how excellent it is. Remember what I said about getting what you pay for? If your hall is relatively narrow you shouldn't have a problem, but if it's wider than average, you should be mindful of a lack of coverage at this front centre position. There may be a need for a *centre fill* loudspeaker or even a closely sited pair of loudspeakers, to cure the problem.

With some of this information in mind, you can start to see what a loudspeaker, or more likely a selection of loudspeakers, might produce for you, in your auditorium. But what of the SPL? Just what size or capacity of loudspeaker should you expect to use? In making this assessment, you first need to be aware of just what levels of sound pressure are found in a range of everyday locations, and then you can make an assessment of what may be needed in your particular space. The following chart will give you some information with which to make comparisons and perhaps some idea of just where your requirement will fall.

All of this still provides no specific rules for just what SPL or arrangement of loudspeakers is needed in any given space. As I have said, it is an exacting science, and experience and often measurements and calculations are needed to assess and specify the correct loudspeaker type and layout, in a given auditorium.

Just to confuse things even further, when you look at the data quoted by a loudspeaker manufacturer, it will say something like 'SPL 120dB @ 1W 1 metre'. This means that the maximum level for 1 Watt input was taken at 1 metre from the loudspeaker. Now I'm sure you can see that this isn't really very helpful, since your seated audience won't be sitting within 1 metre of the loudspeaker and there are two other factors to be considered, in order to make use of this information. Firstly, and remember these are basic rules, each time the power input to the loudspeaker is doubled, 3 dB of SPL is added. Secondly, each time the distance between the loudspeaker and the listener is doubled, the SPL is reduced by 6 dB. So, as you can see, you need to give some careful thought and planning to the selection of loudspeakers in your auditorium.

Leaving aside the specific type and quantity involved in loudspeakers, we've at last come to the starting point of our sound system equipment, the end. It may be the end of the system equipment, but in the hearing process, it's just about the first thing to be considered, I hope you follow the back-to-front logic in all this because, as I said, loudspeakers in the wrong place simply can't do the job, so what to some will seem the last part of the system, is in my opinion really the first and the most critical to get right.

Sound Pressure Levels				
Thresholds	**SPL (dB)**	**Example**		
	180	Rocket Launch		
	140	.45 pistol shot, very near	M	
	130	Thunder clap, air raid siren	U	Loud rock
Threshold of pain	120	Jet plan takeoff at 200' away	S	
	110	Pneumatic road drill, very near	I	
	100	Loud classical music	C	Classical
	90	Manufacturing plant		
	80	Cabin of jet plane cruising	L	
	70	Vacuum cleaner at 10'	E	Background
	60	Average street noise, traffic	V	
	50	Inside a suburban house	E	
	40	A quiet auditorium	L	
	30	Average whisper	S	
	20	Extremely quiet recording studio		
Threshold of hearing	0			

Perhaps you can see now why I made the point about helping those of you with an existing system, and why it's not as simple as taking a snapshot look at just one component part. Now we've got quite a few other areas to cover before we can start to make some sense of it all.

3 COMPATIBLE EQUIPMENT, AMPLIFIERS AND PROCESSING

Let's go back to our simple scenario. You probably have two full range loudspeakers covering your seated area, happy in the knowledge that the coverage and SPL properties are good enough for your needs. But there's a little more to it before we've finished with loudspeakers – the mechanical fixing. Remember you are probably dealing with between 20-30kgs or more in each loudspeaker, even in a relatively small installation, so the fixing suspension point must be given due consideration. The actual mounting bracket, a fixing or suspension bracket that is going to support the loudspeaker to provide both the pan and tilt function, that will be needed to focus the loudspeaker, can sometimes be an expense that you may not have expected. But don't be tempted to skimp on it. It's one of those small seemingly insignificant little things that when added all together will make or break your sound system.

I seem to have gone on for ages about loudspeakers and yet I know I have left so much unsaid. However, it's time for the next element of sound system equipment, the amplifier, and no, in spite of current moves to retro-spec a valve type, it will be a solid state device. Amplifiers are the engine of the system, usually and hopefully a very boring piece of equipment that you simply need to turn on and off. But again, they have to be correctly specified.

I probably should have mentioned this little fact somewhat sooner, but almost all performance related sound systems, are designed and built to provide a stereo (that's left and right) output. Some of you may find this rather odd; after all, there is hardly ever a requirement to provide a true left or right stereo image for a single microphone. This is because it is generally accepted that this one single point sound source, the performer, will be distributed evenly between both the left and right stereo channels. Likewise, the full benefit of a stereo sound signal can really only be appreciated when heard from the centre position. But in any given auditorium only a very small fraction of the audience gets this benefit, so why bother? Well, there will be occasions when a stereo signal may be required. Obviously pre-recorded music is almost bound to be recorded in stereo, but what about something like a sound effect of a car, aeroplane, herd of wildebeest etc, supposedly crossing the stage or auditorium?

Yes, I know there are other ways that you could achieve these effects without it being a stereo recording, but I hope you see the point. Taking things several steps further (some might say a few steps too far), there have been events and uses of quadraphonic sound (four point sources) and cinema auditoriums have subjected us to surround sound, but I think these things have all died out now, or are at least very specialised, leaving us with the regulation stereo two channels. The loudspeakers, of course, are single point sound devices, so you need two to achieve the stereo signal effect.

Most performance related amplifiers are in fact stereo amplifiers: two amplifiers, one dedicated left and one right, neatly packaged into one box. I made some rather caustic remarks about loudspeakers all being black boxes and seemingly the same, no matter which manufacturer they came from. Guess what? The amplifiers are in the same mould.

You will, by now, have spotted my love of making analogies to the motor industry. Well, they all have four wheels, an engine and some seats, and they usually go and stop when you make them. Boring things aren't they? Most of us users have an ongoing love hate relationship with the one we own. We crave for something that looks sexy, sporty, racy, goes faster or makes more noise than the ones your mates have, and the one thing we demand is that they don't break down. Sorry! Am I talking about cars or amplifiers? I've forgotten which!

Remember my criteria for choosing a loudspeaker? Well they are very similar for an amplifier: it must be the correct specification; it must be of proven reliability; but there it stops. The value for money, ease of installation, aesthetics, just aren't important (don't tell the accountant about the value for money bit), because in almost all applications, they are going to get buried inside an equipment rack, and you will hope to only look at them once a year, when you do an electrical test on your equipment.

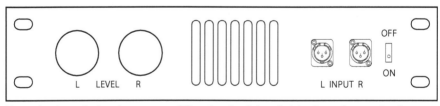

Example of a typical rack-mount amplifier, showing left and right channel output level controllers, cooling slots, left and right channel line inputs and the power switch. The loudspeaker outputs are mounted on the rear of this unit.

But the correct specification? There are two vital things to get right: the maximum power output of the amplifier should be as close as possible to, but not exceeding the maximum rating of the loudspeaker. Be careful, and make sure that you have referenced these figures from the same source, since some manufacturers use the AES reference while some use the RMS value, but both are talking about the same thing, just using different terms of reference, a little like Celsius and Fahrenheit. The point is that an imbalance could present problems, as when someone sets a 500W amplifier to maximum and wrecks the loudspeakers that were only rated at 300W. Or in reverse, is driving the 300W amplifier flat out all of the time, thus to destruction, in trying to generate more sound through the 500W loudspeakers which are only working just over 50% of their potential. The other factor is the *impedance* and again you will find that both the loudspeakers and amplifier will have a listing for their nominal rating, typically either 4 or 8 Ohms.

At this point, and to echo the point about wrecking loudspeakers or destroying amplifiers, I want to introduce you to headroom and another car analogy. The speedometer on my car goes up to 180mph, if I could find a road which was long, empty and straight enough, it might get somewhere near to it, but how long would my car last if I treated it that way? In the real world, we can't and don't need to travel that fast, but we do like to have the capacity on tap for that odd occasion when we need it. And so it is with the power rating of the sound system – far better to be running at 30 to 50% of its maximum potential than at 95% with steam coming out of it! So in putting your system together, leave plenty of headroom in your planning.

In many ways this whole business of how big or how powerful the amplifiers need to be is driven and dictated by the loudspeakers. Typically, you may find that a loudspeaker that will deliver you a good SPL will be rated at 300 / 400 or even 500 Watts, so your amplifier will automatically follow this requirement.

There are a few more important things you need to know and consider about power amplifiers.

1. As the name says they are *power* amplifiers and they will be the biggest consumer of power amongst the many elements of equipment making up your sound system. So, a dedicated power supply will probably be a requirement to the site of the amplifier/s. (More of this later.)

2. In doing the job they do, they often generate heat; so don't expect to lock them in a sealed cupboard.

3. They are often fitted with a fan, for cooling purposes. In some models,

the fan sucks and blows air from front to back, in others, from bottom to top. Again, this is an important factor when you are going to mount the power amplifiers into an equipment rack, where thought must be given to the rack layout.

Even with the modern solid state power amplifier, there are several types, the 'switched mode' type where one of the main benefits, is the weight saving, as opposed to the older more traditional Mosfet (*metal oxide semiconductor field effect transistor*) type, in which part of the electronic circuitry relies on large toroidal transformers, making it much heavier. Whatever the choice there are three functions which all-good amplifiers should have:

Soft start or soft power up: simply have a built-in function that turns on the internal components of the amplifier in stages.

DC Protection, so that in the event of a component failure, no harmful DC voltages can be output, causing expensive damage to the loudspeakers.

Signal or Clip Limiters: govern the output of the amplifier, to reduce the likelihood of distorted sound if the amplifier is being overdriven.

On top of these essentials, I would expect a power amplifier to have 3 pin XLR sockets to provide connection for inputs to both left and right channels, possibly with standard ¼″ Jack sockets connected in parallel with the XLRs and the left and right outputs of the amplifier to be in Speakon NL4 outlets, this now being the industry standard connector for loudspeaker wiring. Some amplifiers will carry level or volume controls on the front panel, some may only have a screwdriver setting for level/volume on the rear panel, not visible or accessible to meddling fingers. The choice is yours, depending on your needs.

The mention of loudspeaker wiring brings me to yet another of those critical component parts of a sound system, one that is usually and regularly overlooked by most people. Remember my comments about the weakest link? Well, here we have it again, expensive and well specified loudspeakers, and amplifiers of a similar pedigree, all linked together with a small low value piece of twin flex, that would have a problem running power to your front door bell! No, in loudspeaker wiring there is simply no substitute for a good-sized copper conductor. I don't like making general statements for things like this but I would never expect to see loudspeaker wiring specified at less than 2.5sq mm and on long runs of 50m+, probably 4 or 6sq mm. The hi-fi fraternity will promote very high-grade oxygen free cable. All I will say here is that we are not dealing with a hi-fi system, we are dealing with performance sound and different rules and specifications apply. So, getting the loudspeaker wiring (cable) correct is another of those vital weakest link points that just has to be right.

On a technical note, by way of explanation, the actual power output of a typical stereo amplifier is something in the order of 70V, and if you run this over any distance, say 20m, and run it down a low value (small size) piece of cable, the voltage 'drop', the voltage lost when the signal gets to the other end of the cable and connects to the loudspeaker, is appreciable. So much so in fact, that to compensate, you will find that you need to increase the level (turn up the amplifier) to get the desired sound level. In the worst case, as in a very long cable run and a very small size cable, you could reach a point where you can't increase the level enough. At this point, you are stressing the component parts of your system, the power amplifier, which is being driven harder than necessary and indeed the loudspeaker wiring, which will probably start to get warm! The audio signal will become distorted and all for the want of a correctly sized piece of cable, which probably only cost a few pence more overall.

While we are on the subject of loudspeaker wiring, I said that the power amplifier should have a Speakon NL4 outlet, well, all wiring for loudspeakers, whether at the amplifier, loudspeaker or intermediate patch position should, in my opinion, be terminated in this industry standard connector. They are designed specifically for terminating loudspeaker wiring. They are robust and can't be easily confused with anything else in your performance space, so use them and be happy that the industry has found and settled on one thing that really works well.

I said a little earlier that sound systems are designed around a 'stereo' characteristic, and our school hall scenario thus far has been talking about one pair of loudspeakers working in our auditorium, using one stereo amplifier to power them. It's rather unusual, but not unknown, for a performance sound system to stop at just one pair of loudspeakers and one amplifier. It may be that the auditorium needs a second or third pair of loudspeakers; the system may need the addition of sub bass loudspeakers and fold-back loudspeakers (on stage or in an orchestra pit), and each time you add loudspeakers, you will also be adding amplifiers to power them. Thus is born the need for a loudspeaker patch.

In many performance spaces, it is common to find a fairly high number of loudspeaker outlets, especially around the stage and maybe the orchestra pit if there is one, to enable the users to connect loudspeakers at convenient points, dictated by the requirements of the production taking place at the time. For example, a production might call for sound effects to be heard off stage, or for foldback on stage for artists and musicians. All of this brings a need to have additional loudspeaker outlets and wiring, and the wiring will of course all end up back at the location of the power amplifiers where the loudspeaker patch will be located.

Almost all professional power amplifiers have their mains power switch and volume controls on the front panel and their inputs and outputs on the rear panel. A following chapter will describe equipment racks, where things like the power amplifiers will be sited. The loudspeaker patch is simply a panel, normally found on the front of an equipment rack adjacent to the power amplifiers. This panel will contain any number of Speakon NL4 sockets, some being connected to the output of the amplifiers, some being connected to the wiring going to the various locations of loudspeakers and loudspeaker outlets all around the venue. These input and output connectors will be set up with keyway orientation that will prevent the accidental connection of the output from one power amplifier to be connected to another. The patch also provides flexibility, in that you can decide which power amplifier is designated to which loudspeaker. This also provides an element of safety back-up as, in the unlikely event of an amplifier failing during a performance, were it also in a critical position, i.e. driving the main auditorium loudspeakers, it could be re-patched and replaced by using an amplifier from a less critical area, all by means of a few patch cables, in a few seconds.

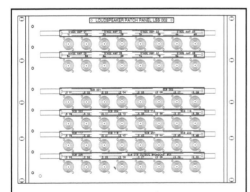

Example of a loudspeaker patch rack. The top two rows of Speakon connectors are the amplifier outputs, and the bottom four rows are connected to the various loudpeakers around the hall. The connection from amplifier to loudspeaker is made by a short patch lead between the chosen amplifier and loudspeaker.

I hope you have noticed how we are steadily working backwards in our equipment chain, loudspeakers, loudspeaker wiring and connectors, loudspeaker patch, and power amplifiers. We are almost at the point where we might get some sort of sound to come out of our sound system, but not yet, for there are several more elements to go.

Ten years ago, or for the unconverted, last week, we may have been about to delve into the good old (but nowadays old-fashioned) Graphic Equaliser – known as the EQ for short – another of those magic little black boxes that can have a drastic and often beneficial effect on your sound system. The old EQ is often described as having so many 'bands' usually either 16 or 32 and each band is in fact a frequency filter, often built as a two channels or stereo unit. The EQ unit is used to treat and modify the sound signal prior to its input into the amplifier, so yet again we are going back another step up the equipment chain. I said we may have been going to delve into the Graphic Equaliser, then described it rather unkindly as old-fashioned, the reason being that modern technology has brought us something better, in fact much better: the DSP the Digital Signal Processor. This will provide all the functions found within the old Graphic Equaliser plus other functions, such as Parametric EQ, Delay, Compression, Limiting, and probably a few others that I have forgotten. The point is, that all of these functions are now contained in an even smaller little black box and, more importantly, they are accessed, addressed, set-up, monitored, and stored by connecting the DSP to your computer. Many of the latest DSPs have some wonderful tools that come with them to help you set up your system. For instance, when you are setting up your system, let's go back to our simple scenario of the full range loudspeakers in the school hall. With at least one model you set the DSP to output a test signal, known as 'pink noise'. You then provide the DSP with a microphone input, the microphone being in the hall listening to the pink noise. The DSP then automatically sets up the EQ of your hall, increasing and decreasing the individual filters, as you may have done manually with the old EQ unit, but with a more accurate end product.

I may have simplified, even glorified the functions of the DSP over the simple Graphic Equaliser, but believe me, they are so much better; but then they do cost two or three times as much as the old EQ.

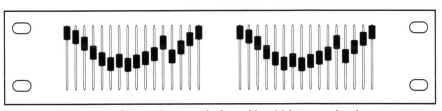

Example of a stereo graphic equaliser - each channel has 16 frequency bands.

I said that the EQ or indeed the DSP is used to modify the signal prior to its amplification, then I started using a series of words (Parametric EQ, Delay, Compression, Limiting) and although as a global description, they do all modify the signal on one way or another. It's probably a good idea for you to understand just what these modifications are, and why you might need them, so here goes, in layman's terms I promise:

Parametric EQ: A Graphic Equaliser, where the bandwidth (the range of frequencies) and the individual frequencies, are both adjustable.

Delay: The act of 'delaying' a signal, used to compensate for physical distance in a hall or auditorium, where the loudspeakers are at a distance from each other.

Compression/Limiting: A device which limits the dynamic range of an audio signal, usually at the top or bottom of its range.

Before the advent of the modern DSP, all of these modification tools were, and in fact still are, available to you as an individual stand-alone item. The real question is knowing what's on offer, and do you actually need any of it? Well, for venues that need a delay within the loudspeaker system, you really don't have much choice, because to leave it out will seriously compromise the intelligibility level of the whole system. The rest? Well, in a simple system you probably won't need it, since their use is getting too far away from the *basic* premise of this book, so I won't dwell on them much longer, except to say that, if you spend the money on a decent DSP, these functions will be there, as you and your system users develop a need for them.

4 THE SPAGHETTI FACTOR!

There's something about the technical side of the performing arts, especially the lighting and, even more so, the sound, which dictates that, unless it looks a real mess and has bundles of wires hanging out of everything in sight, it just can't be the 'real' job. Somehow it's almost expected, even demanded that it should look this way. I don't subscribe to this, and certainly not in a permanent fixed installation. Of course, if you are dealing with something designed to tour – setting up in a different place each week or night – one accepts a degree of messy flexibility, but getting back to our simple scenario and the school hall, it can and should be neat and tidy, with the minimum amount of 'spaghetti' cabling visible to the audience and the user!

One factor in achieving this is the humble equipment rack. In today's world, about 95% of all the equipment you will use at the control position is supplied in, or can be adapted to, a rack mounting format. Some explanation about the rack is needed. The standard British equipment rack is one of those devices that is always talked about as being 19″ (that's inches) wide, never 495mm, due to its American origins. Its other dimensions are referenced in millimetres, including its depth and 'U' factors, which are actually 45mm (1¾″) for its height, so we end up talking about a 19″ rack being 24U high and, unless it has a specific need to house deep section equipment, the depth factor isn't mentioned at all, until you get it on site and find that the equipment won't fit in! That's when you know you need a deep section version! By the way, just to confuse you completely, I've been saying it's 19″ wide, when actually it's an inch or two wider than that, the 19″ bit refers to the aperture at the front and rear, into which the 19″ rack mounting equipment, of all types, will fit.

I'm not sure if the equipment manufacturers caused the racks to be built in these dimensions, or if there was a world mountain of 19″racks which caused the manufacturers to build all their equipment to suit, but whichever way it happened, as I've said the vast majority of the things you will need to use are built to be rack mounted. The result of which is that, except for the sound mixer, and even these can be rack mounted in their smaller versions, all of the things you need can be contained in a nice metal cabinet, presenting the front operating panel of the equipment facing you and, just as importantly, providing the opportunity to keep all of the spaghetti under control and mostly hidden away inside the back of the rack.

If you haven't experienced the ordered uniformity of having your sound equipment laid out in equipment racks, or even if you have experienced the mess and chaos of fifteen different component parts individually strewn across your worktop, plus that spaghetti, then take it from me – the equipment rack is a must.

In a small set up, like our school hall scenario, it would be possible to fit all of the various components of equipment into one equipment rack, but when you pause to analyse what you are doing, you may find that's not the best plan.

The equipment will split into two distinct categories: the hands on and the hands off. The source equipment is what I usually describe as hands on, such as CD players, Mini Disc players, cassette tape players, effects processors, radio microphone receivers, patch fields etc. Anything and everything that you will need to get your hands on at some time during the performance. The 'hands off' equipment is located in the 'power handling' rack and is more or less everything else: amplifiers, DSPs, loudspeaker patch, and various other items, from other technical disciplines, that will find their way into the equipment rack for convenience. It will follow that the hands on rack will need to be at the nerve centre, control and operation position, next to the sound mixer, and in fingertip reach of the sound operator. The hands off rack may be somewhere near to the control position, but may be at the other end of the building, since once it's turned on, you should have little cause to get your hands on it during the performance – famous last words.

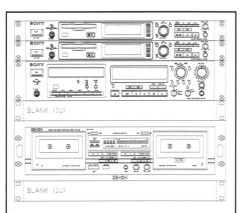

Example of a source equipment rack. This one houses two mini disk players, a CD player and a double cassette deck. 2U of this rack are spare and are covered over with standard U blank plates.

When talking about amplifiers, I made the point about a power supply being available, noting that there was more to follow. Here it is, and yet another of those critical important factors that must be right.

In the small to medium size

venue, our school hall, the total amount of power (amperage) needed to run the sound system equipment could be drawn from a local 13A ring main. Sadly however, in my experience, this is often the case, whereas to do the job properly, the sound system equipment needs a dedicated power supply. It's not the size of the supply that's the vital factor; it's the *nature* of the supply. Let me try to explain.

In any building, new or old, there will be many electrical systems in place, some simple, like general lighting in rooms and corridors, some more complex, like the performance lighting. Then there may be an air management plant, involving air conditioning or cooling equipment, general power, office equipment; the list and types of equipment is vast. Some of the equipment used may well affect or produce interference with your sound system. For instance, the performance lighting does its job by changing the normal AC (alternating current) waveform of the power supply. Other equipment, such as motors stopping and starting within the air conditioning plant, or the chiller units in the bar, may also cause what are known as *spikes* . All of this is of no consequence to the actual equipment in use, but some of this interference can seriously affect the performance of your sound system equipment if it is connected to a power supply derived from the same source.

In recent years, there has been some useful legislation put in place to attempt to resolve this problem and, in general, electrical equipment now has to conform to these regulations (see The EMC Directive).

However, the situation still exists, despite the regulations, that within your typical electrical installation, your mains power supply could be another of those small problems that adversely affects the working of your sound equipment system. The best plan is to source the power directly from the distribution panel at the building intake. In making specifications for sound system mains power, I use the following statement:

*'The mains power supply, being ** Amps, SP+N (single phase plus neutral plus earth) shall be derived from the building intake, not a local distribution panel, and shall provide a 'clean' earth, not being cross bonded with any other part of the wiring infrastructure, but being bonded directly to the main earth point of the building'.*

If you have achieved this then you should at least have a 'clean' starting point on which to base your sound equipment.

So, another step on the ladder, and we now have a clean power supply feeding our equipment racks and power amplifiers. But in order to make complete sense of it all, there's another of those little black boxes that you really should consider: the mains power distribution, which provides a number of functions:

1   To provide enough physical places to connect all the various parts of the equipment to the mains power supply.

2   To provide a degree of 'mains power conditioning' to protect against things like over voltage, mains spikes etc, since different units may provide different functions.

3   To provide a sequential 'power up' and 'power down' facility, ensuring that your equipment is turned on and off in the correct order, thus helping to prevent bangs and thumps from the loudspeakers.

There are several manufacturers who build mains power distribution units, which also provide the sequential power up/power down function. Again, these items are also seemingly insignificant things that you may not have budgeted for, costing anything from £150 to £450, depending on the type and specification. But again I would urge you not to condemn them out of hand in favour of the ubiquitous 4-way 13A blocks in multiple, probably all feeding from each other. It's another of those small things, the inclusion or omission of which, can and will make a difference to the overall performance of your sound system, one way or the other!

5 PATCHES AND FACILITY PANELS

We've really been moving on in the equipment chain within our school hall scenario. We have loudspeakers, the brackets that hold them in place, the connectors and the loudspeaker wiring, loudspeaker patch, amplifiers, DSP units, equipment racks and power distribution, and even the specification for a clean power supply.

Surely we must be getting somewhere near to the epicentre of the sound system, 'the mixer' almost? But I need to prolong the waiting just a little longer. I want to skip over the mixer at the moment, but it's important, vital, the heart of all sound systems, so I promise I will come back to it. Since I expect you will all appreciate what the mixer does within the overall working of your sound system, I want to consider just a few other elements of hardware first, even though they are actually on the other side of the mixer, the input side.

Consider what you are going to feed into your sound mixer: all sorts of sound signals, some as a single or mono signal, as in a microphone, some as a stereo signal from a CD playing pre-recorded music. Even in a small system, I suggest that you will be surprised at just how many signals will be involved. Now, you could of course bring all of these various signals (cables) to the mixer position (another bundle of spaghetti), have them all terminated in the relevant connectors and connect them into the mixer as and when needed.

Alternatively you could bring all these signals back to one position adjacent to the mixer and terminate them all into one large 'patch field' together with all the inputs and outputs of the mixer. There are a number of types of patch field available to you, but still the most popular is probably the 'jack patch'. Jack connectors, plugs and sockets come in a variety of types and sizes. The industry standard for the jack patch is the GPO 'B' gauge type. This will provide you with the opportunity to build your 'patch' in rows of either 20 or 24 jack sockets per row, and as many rows as you like. They are neat, tidy, robust, and rarely, if ever, go wrong. They also have a little trick which other forms of patch panel connectors can't achieve – something called 'normalising'. This is where a signal is brought into the jack patch and without any patch cable being used, it is routed out straight to a designated channel of the mixing desk, and only when a patch lead is inserted is the signal first disconnected from its 'normal'

A GPO Jack Patch in construction.

routing, to be patched by the user into a different destination of their choosing. Patching, normalising, and all that's involved, takes quite a bit of planning, even on a small simple system, so unless you have had experience of it, my advise would be to leave it to someone who has, but to keep you sane, neat and tidy, it's another of those things you really should have as a *vital* part of your sound system. Yet another note of caution is needed here. When considering the make-up of a signal patch, I have said that the standard is a GPO B gauge type jack connector, but there are other types available e.g. the 'A' type, which is an inferior specification to the 'B', usually being a cheaper plastic body type product. Don't be tempted to save a few pounds; pay the money and buy the best!

As a consequence of adopting a patch panel into your system, you will, by default, also need to supply dedicated sound signal wiring in and out of it. All of the wiring from microphones, CD, mini disc, cassette, effects processors etc will need to connect to it, as will almost every input and output and connection facility found on the sound mixer. You will quickly see the numbers of patch ways rising, even if you are only using a relatively small mixer of, say, 12 or 16 input channels and perhaps 4 sub groups and a main left and right output, and obviously the wiring associated with all this just begets even more of that spaghetti!

At various positions around the performance space, it is usual to provide a number of connection points for all of the equipment used with and in association with your sound system. Obviously microphones and loudspeakers, when used at floor level, are a good example, but there may well be quite a few other things, such as communication headsets, cue lights, DMX512 connection, ethernet connection, paging system microphone, composite video connection, CCTV – BNC connection etc. There is really no standard format, it's whatever combination of facilities you use in your venue, hence the term 'facility panel'.

These panels, there may be just a couple or, in larger venues, there may be 20 or 30 or more, provide all the required connectivity in a neat and ordered style. They can be finished in styles and colours to suit the surroundings, and may be built as flush fixing for a new build, or surface fixing for existing buildings. Similar panels can also provide connection for performance lighting (dimmer) outlets, local 13A ring main outlets, larger mains power outlets, motor controls etc. However, in light of electrical regulations governing the termination and containment of electrical wiring, it is generally accepted that all mains voltage (230V) terminations are kept separate from what is generally described as 'low voltage' wiring, meaning practically everything else. Anyway, with reference my comments about electrical interference when talking about the mains power supply for your sound system – you don't want to be mixing the sound signal wiring with mains wiring.

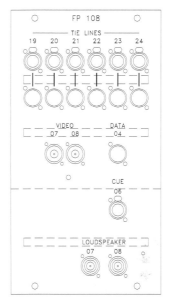

Typical 'facilities' panel showing audio tie lines, video and loudspeaker outlets.

If you were to reduce the requirement, to connect only microphones (inputting) and loudspeakers (outputting) to your sound system equipment, you could use a sound signal multicore cable for the microphones and run individual two-core cables to each loudspeaker. This method has obvious advantages, where systems are configured in different styles and locations, as in a touring set up, or even in a static venue where the equipment has to serve different rooms within it. The disadvantages of this method are perhaps not quite so obvious. It will take time to run out and set up all the cables involved. Generally it never looks very pretty to see the venue draped with loose cable running all over the place, and lastly, in these days of Health and Safety legislation, you are very likely to create a trip hazard or simply not be allowed to festoon cables over the top of doorways. So within most permanent venues, a degree of fixed wiring, the infrastructure of the sound system, will be a requirement, and the facility panel is needed to terminate it all.

Much of the wiring involved in the facility panels will be wired into one or other of the equipment racks I have promoted in chapter 4, where it will be terminated into either the jack patch or the loudspeaker patch. Again I find myself using the same boring old comment about people not realising the importance or cost of what some may regard as an insignificant, even un-called for addition to the hardware of the sound system, and again making reference to the importance of each facet of the system adding to the overall success of it.

On the subject of wiring, and I used the term 'infrastructure of the sound system', it's worth a note here that, even though you may regard the sound system wiring as a fairly low key requirement, it still needs to be installed, as do all electrical installation works, to the standards laid down by the IEE (Institute of Electrical Engineers) who issue a standard, currently the 16th edition, of wiring regulations. This is a specialist field of expertise, which I am not going to attempt to involve you with in this book. My reason for mentioning it here is that you should understand the ramifications of 'correct' electrical installation works.

Sadly, it is often the case that where sound equipment has been installed into an existing building, rather than as a part of the build programme from new, it is installed in a less than correct manner. The main visible parts of a sound system wiring installation are usually the loudspeaker wiring and the microphone signal wiring, often just clipped to the walls and ceilings of the building. This wiring, as with all other installed electrical wiring, should properly be within a containment of either metal conduit or trunking for the majority of its length. If you are dealing with a new build project, then the method and application of an electrical installation, in this case a sound system, will almost certainly be under the control of the building programme and will be undertaken in accordance with all the relevant electrical regulations. However, if you are involved in an existing building, where the sound system infrastructure is to be installed in isolation, be cautious that the installation is carried out in the correct manner, not just a few cables clipped loosely to the building structure. A bona fide electrical contractor should provide you with a *completion certificate*, which will state that the installation design and the installation itself have been carried out compliant with the IEE regulations. It should also provide you with test results for the wiring installed, which is often regarded as an integral part of a building's suitability to be granted a performance licence, issued by a local authority or council, in conjunction with the local fire service authority. So it can be a very important thing to get right.

In discussing signal wiring, it's a term used usually to describe everything other than the loudspeaker wiring, although of course to be perfectly correct the loudspeaker wiring is also carrying a sound signal. You will hear people talking about 'balanced' or 'unbalanced' lines, and in today's world virtually 100% of signal wiring is balanced. Unless you are dealing with a very old and poorly specified system, you will probably never come across any unbalanced wiring.

In a balanced signal wiring system, each circuit, e.g. a microphone, has a twin-screened cable; the two signal cores carry the signal and the screen carries no signal. The piece of equipment that you are connecting the signal into (i.e. sound mixer channel) will reference the 'interference' in the two signal wires, and by what is known as common mode rejection, will cancel out, or, as the name implies, balance the signal. The screen wire, carrying no signal, is often wrongly referred to as earth, when it's correct reference is 'ground'. (Earth is a term referenced to electrical safety, whereas ground is a point of 0 voltage in a circuit or system)

Just for your reference, in the unbalanced wiring system there would be only one signal core cable with a screen and the signal would use the screen as its signal return wire. This method is synonymous with noise and interference, which is why it's not used now in professional sound systems.

The majority of signal wiring, indeed all signal wiring associated with microphones, will use a metal body, 3 pin XLR connector (originally manufactured by Cannon),

where:

Pin 1 is connected to the screen.

Pin 2 is connected to the red (sometimes *referred to as 'hot' or +*) cable, and

Pin 3 is connected to the blue (sometimes *referred to as the 'cold' or* -) cable.

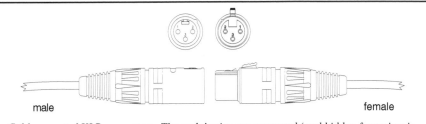

male   female

Cable mounted XLR connectors. The male's pins are protected (and hidden from view in the drawing) by the casing, and the female latches into it for a secure connection. The female can only be removed by pressing down on the latch mechanism. Notice how the pins align in the end-view drawings above.

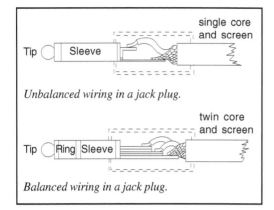

Unbalanced wiring in a jack plug.

Balanced wiring in a jack plug.

Where signal wiring is connected using a jack plug connection, as in the case of the signal patch, then the jack plug is often referred to as a TRS (Tip – Ring – Sleeve) or stereo jack where the tip is the left channel (red wire) connection, the ring is the right channel (blue wire) connection and the sleeve or chassis of the plug is the connection point for the screen.

In a professional sound system set up, the type of Jack plug we are dealing with is called a standard jack. The smaller, 3mm and 5mm diameter jack plugs, are often referred to as mini jacks and are not widely used in a professional sound environment.

Signal wiring terminations for other various items of equipment will usually either be 3 pin XLR, Standard TRS Jack, or in multiple mono connectors called *phono* plugs. These are only for a mono signal (one half of a stereo signal), and will only have one centre pin and the case or chassis of the connector for wiring connection.

The actual signal wiring cable is another area which can provide yet another 'weakest' link. Both the signal wiring between microphone connection points, which may be at some distance form the sound mixer, and the signal wiring between the sound source and processing equipment and the mixer – indeed not forgetting such mundane things as microphone connection cables. All need to be of a good quality with a high specification of both the conductors and, just as importantly, the screen element of the cable. I don't propose to get into the detail and technical specification of what's on offer in the world of cable, but yet again the price will tell you the same old story, so don't skimp on it.

6 THE CONTROL POSITION AND MIXER

We must be about half way through the minefield of what constitutes a sound system and the perils of putting the component parts together, and I am constantly wrestling with my dilemma of what to include, what to concentrate on and what not to mention at all, because of the confusion it may cause. All this coupled with my assuming perhaps too much of you my reader, in terms of the general level of understanding of what the norms are in a performance sound system. I have been blandly rambling on, about all sorts of technical bits and pieces, while assuming that you will have the same mind's eye overview of a sound system layout as I have. All of which brings me to my next assumption. Let's see if you agree.

The control position – the site of the mixer and sound operator I have already described as the nerve centre – is vitally important. Let's stick with our school hall scenario, as this will probably give us the opportunity to explore both ends of the spectrum, as far as the control position is concerned.

I will say that in any performance related space, there is a need for a dedicated technical area, or control position and in dealing with the requirements of sound, this has to be in a FOH (Front of House) position, not tucked away in a storeroom on the side of the stage. If we are dealing with a traditionally shaped hall set out for end stage performance work, or even in a studio or black box type environment, I will promote the dedicated control position. This type of position can take many forms, a room outside the hall possibly with a window or aperture looking into the hall from high level, maybe a dedicated section of a balcony within the hall at the opposite end of the performance stage, possibly a temporary scaffolding structure within the hall, maybe nothing more than an area of floor space at the rear of the hall cordoned off for technical use only. I said we would explore both ends of the spectrum, well if you're lucky your hall will have a dedicated control room, if you're not, you will be working from the flat floor at the rear of the hall. We'll start with the dedicated control room.

So, you would think life's nice and easy in here, your own separate room, probably not quite big enough, but you can't have everything. So you can have a work top surface to fill full of equipment, you probably have to share the space with the lighting control operator and maybe a followspot or two, but you're all technicians and this is your little kingdom. If you're really lucky you will actually be able to see the stage area, but most important of all for the sound mixer, can you hear the auditorium? And I do mean the auditorium.

Here comes another of my often-used phrases: "you can't mix live sound from behind a piece of glass; you have to have the ambient sound of the auditorium at the mixer position."

The reason for this is quite simple and is all to do with the live aspect of what you are doing. At some point, the live element of work will involve a performer using a microphone, this being connected to the mixing desk at the control position and under your control, for you will set the level (volume) of the microphone in use. All microphones, some more than others, can produce what is called feedback if the level (volume) is set too high; this is because the microphone is effectively listening to itself.

Think of the chain of events – the microphone is picking up sound frequencies from the performer, but also picking up some of the background or ambient sound in the hall. This is then fed via the mixer into the amplifier, where the signal is boosted, amplified and sent to the loudspeakers, which puts the sound back into the hall, where the process of gathering frequencies through the microphone starts all over again. There will come a point when, if the level (volume) of the microphone is set too high, a high pitched ringing or whistling sound is generated. This is feedback.

It follows, that in the mixing of live performance sound, it is absolutely vital that the person doing the mixing job can hear the actual sound existing within the hall and, as my often-used phrase says, not from behind a piece of glass. It is simply not possible to do the mixing job with any degree of accuracy and avoid the feedback situation if you are forced to work this way. No, small monitor loudspeakers or worse still, headphones are not the answer – they only make the problem worse by giving a false sound, which is different from that within the hall. They may be useful for other reasons but are definitely not a cure for working in a control room with a sealed window. If you stop and think about seeing a professional production in a theatre or large arena, you will almost certainly remember seeing the sound mixing position within the seated area at the rear of the hall, sometimes even in the middle of the seats. This is the reason why, and there's no getting away from it.

So the control position or room must have a large opening window, the bigger the better, so that the sound mixer operator has a chance of getting the mix level correct in the hall. Obviously the feedback issue is only one part of all this. The mixer operator needs to gauge the overall level of sound and, where needed, apply higher or lower levels to individual performers as the needs of each and the production dictate.

In the other control position scenario, my concerns about hearing the sound from the auditorium will not be a problem, since you are likely to be sitting in it. So the hearing problem is solved, but many other issues may turn into problems as a consequence of having no dedicated room or area to be the technical centre for all of the equipment involved. You should remember, as I noted in the control room condition, that other technical disciplines bring equipment and personnel to this position, so there are many things to be considered.

Even if there are just two people, one lighting, one sound, there will be some degree of sound or noise generated, the low level chatter on the technical communications ring equipment, the loading and unloading of CD, mini disc or cassette machines, the general moving about of the two operators in their work and the fact that at least some of the area will need to be lit so that the operators can see what they are doing, when all around them are sitting in almost total darkness. Perhaps you can see the distractions involved. Of course, if what you are doing is a fairly loud and raucous event, like a musical or pantomime, it probably won't be an issue at all, but it could be very different if it were a heavy piece of wordy drama. As if these considerations were not enough, you also have to think about the Health and Safety issues that will arise. In putting technical equipment and personnel into a public auditorium space, you may find you are very restricted in what you are allowed to do. I can't offer much of a solution here, except to say, make sure you check out your intended set-up with due regard to Health and Safety and local authority legislation, before you put it all in place, because if you don't, and you are forced to move it all, it could ruin your day, not to mention the production.

So, with some sort of control position sorted out, we can at last assess the requirements for the central piece for sound equipment, the mixer. I've described it as vital and of course it is, as it is the one item of equipment that you, the operator, will be using all the time. Please don't forget my comments about the weakest link, the sound mixer being just one link in the chain, but for lots of people who have to use the sound system, the functions provided by the mixing desk are very important, from the users' viewpoint. There are many considerations here: the number of channels available; the EQ section, the number of auxiliary outputs and their orientation, the routing of the signal path and how many sub and main outputs are available, the desk layout and the inclusion of VU (Volume Unit) meters or the more modern, but perhaps less accurate, PPM (Peak Progress Meters); and perhaps last but not least, the cost of the thing.

I said somewhere earlier, when talking about loudspeakers, that one thing that might help in assessing the available options, would be the cost and the fact that the more you pay the better the product is likely to be, and within the realms of sound mixing desks there is a very good reason for this. Yes, the actual desk element of the mixer could be built to a higher standard, with a more robust font metal panel that doesn't bend when you touch it and the end cheeks could be made in a nice polished wood, and the lower front section could be extended with a padded section, making it more comfortable to operate. But none of that is as important as the fact that if you pay more for it, the circuitry inside it will be built to a higher standard, there will be a higher specification of components used, all of which will bring about one very important end result: the mixer will generate less noise – that's unwanted noise from its own component parts, giving you a better end product. Others better qualified and more technical than me, and no doubt all of the manufacturers, will give you masses of data to support their case, but the basic information you need to know is never more bound up in the cost, than in the case of the mixing desk's value for money.

Some of you will ask, what about the mixer/amplifier? This is a combination set-up, which packages both the mixer and the amplifier into one unit. This is done for two reasons: firstly to save money, and secondly to provide a simple solution, making life easier where small temporary systems are needed. I'm not a big fan of the combination mixer/amplifier, although I do accept they have their uses in the right circumstances. The problem I have with them is that they make certain elements of the sound system job very difficult, if not impossible to achieve. In this format the output of the mixer is fed directly to the input of the amplifier, so you have no opportunity of introducing a DSP or a graphic EQ into the system. Some manufacturers have tried to resolve this issue by including a graphic EQ section within the mixer. For me this just compounds the problem – you are now putting three things into one unit. I have seen one such multi-function piece of equipment that also included a cassette player – where could it all end? No, in what I will describe as a 'proper' sound system, the mixing desk is just that, and it should perform no other function but to mix, modify, and route the sound signal fed into it.

I used two other descriptive functions in my last statement. Now, we can probably all take as read the mixing function, but to modify and route may need a little explanation for the basic user.

The 'modify' part can happen in a number of ways, the simplest being within the individual channel EQ (Equalisation) section, where the top, middle, and bottom frequencies can be modified, increased or decreased, to achieve the desired result. Or the signal of an individual channel could be selected via one of the auxiliary *send* controls, its signal being sent out of the mixer into a separate piece of equipment, such as an effects processor, be modified and then returned to the mixer, via what are called, unsurprisingly, *auxiliary returns*. Most mixers will have several separate auxiliary sends and returns. Some will be designated 'pre' fader and some 'post' fader, as this would imply some permit access to the channel before the master channel fader and the others after the channel fader. The use and requirement of this will become evident as you grow more accustomed to the overall use of the mixer and all of its functions.

The 'route' part is a user-selectable function, usually one or more small buttons located at the top end of the channel fader, saying something like 1 & 2, 3 & 4 and possibly L & R (Left and Right). This assumes that your sound mixer has what are called *sub group* outputs (1 – 2 – 3 – 4). If the mixer has no sub groups and the output is sent to the main left and right outputs, then it's not likely to have any form of route function.

So we have started to describe some of the functionality of the mixer, and I'm not about to go much further, remembering it's the *basics* I am interested in helping you understand as to why the component parts of the system have to be in place, and not necessarily the whole explanation of how to use them to their fullest potential. That will come with use, your experimentation and perhaps reading books and authors who can do a far better job than me. But to complete my very small exposure of what the sound mixing desk has to offer, I will cite just a couple of other things that may confuse the fist-time novice user.

The connections into and out of the mixer can look almost as daunting as all the knobs and faders on the front panel, especially where some of them seem to be labelled the same, i.e. each channel may appear to have two inputs, but why? Which one is the right one to use? The answer is, because it needs two and both will be used, in the correct circumstances. Confused? The two inputs to the same channel are simply to enable the connection of source signals at different levels of impedance, and they are easy to tell apart, indeed most mixers will actually have them marked 'Mic' (microphone) and 'Line' (virtually everything else) So that's easy, all microphones get connected into the mic input which is normally a 3 pin XLR panel mount socket, while all the other source signals go into the line input which is almost always a standard ¼" stereo Jack socket.

You may find a small push-in switch next to the mic input of each channel or, on smaller mixers, one global selector switch that is marked 'Phantom Power' or simply 'Phantom', or even '48V'. This function applies a small voltage (max 48V) from the mixer onto the selected channel or all channels. This voltage is required to provide power (*phantom power*) to a range of microphones known as *condenser* microphones, which require this small voltage in order to work. We will deal with microphones a little later on, but don't worry about this mixer function; it won't do any harm to other microphones that don't happen to need the voltage.

Several times I have mentioned the 'channel fader'. This is the slider control nearest to you at the bottom of the mixer and it is the main, hands on, control for setting the level of an individual channel. Don't be confused to find another control that appears to duplicate this, this will be a small rotary pot (potentiometer) which is easier to call a pot, right at the top of the mixer, just about as far away as it's possible to get, from the main slider (proper name 'linear') fader.

The linear fader will be marked in a dB (decibel) scale and somewhere near

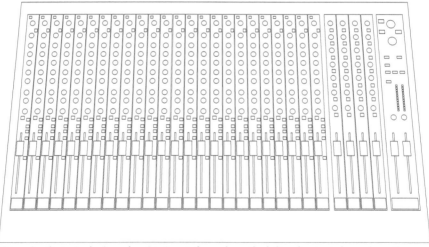

Example of a typical mixer showing input channels on the left and output channels on the right.

the top of its travel, but not the very top, you will see the marking say 00dB: this is probably the optimum operating position for that channel, if we assume a microphone is in use. The pot fader, sometimes called the 'master gain control', will probably be marked in a simple scale of 1 – 10 and again, assuming a microphone is in use, you will set the level (volume) so that with the linear fader set at 00dB, the microphone is below the feedback level.

These two controls, the pot and the linear fader used in conjunction will thus allow you to set a general level (volume) while you will be able to adjust the 'critical' level with the linear fader, as the need arises.

Associated with the master gain pot (next to it) you may find another of those small push-in switches marked -10dB or -20dB. This can sometimes be very useful, as its selection will remove or cut a level of 10/20dB from the signal present in that channel. Where a microphone is concerned, this has two beneficial effects, one being to delay the onset of feedback, the other to remove some, but never all, of what is known as handling noise – especially annoying if you have a performer who either constantly taps or fiddles with the microphone or is just simply rough with it.

Finally, the output section of the mixer. A while back, I talked about groups and routing of the signal to groups. Again it is a very useful function, indeed vital within most sound system applications. Just as with the input channel of a mixer where you want to have the individual control of a sound source, when it comes to the output, something similar is needed. If we go back to our school hall scenario and think about one pair of loudspeakers feeding the output of our sound mixer via the processing and amplification equipment into the hall, it's easy to see that our stereo signal (remember that's left and right) can be controlled by simply the left and right master output faders of the mixer. But what happens when you need to have another output from the mixer, feeding into a different area, at a different level, fulfilling a different requirement, maybe a different area of the auditorium, such as an under balcony infill, or foldback to the stage or orchestra, or a feed for a recording? Then a mixer that has multiple Sub Groups is exactly what you want. Obviously, each individual output 1 – 2 – 3 – 4 and maybe Left & Right as well, will feed into separate dedicated amplifiers via the appropriate DSP processing. What you end up with is a system that gives you instant fingertip control of sound into many different areas of your venue, a very powerful tool in the hands of a skilled sound operator.

To finish with mixers, let me say there are many different types: big small, simple, complex, analogue, digital, rack mounting; the choice and permutations are endless. The one thing they have in common, is that they are all relatively delicate pieces of electronic circuitry and they don't like cigarette ash or liquids being tipped into them, so where you are able, ban smoking, drinking, eating etc anywhere near them, or else you can expect a noisy mixer and sound system and regular expensive repairs.

7 SOURCE EQUIPMENT

By source equipment, I am referring to anything and everything that produces a sound signal – except microphones, which I think you will agree are rather a special case, so we will deal with them separately. In the interests of brevity I'm also going to include effects processors in this section, even though they *modify* rather than *produce* sound.

I made the point a while ago, but within this selection of equipment, I don't think there is anything that's not 19″ rack-mountable. These days, if it doesn't come ready rack mounted, there will be a rack mount kit of metalwork to make it so. Remember my plea for the use of the equipment rack, to resolve the spaghetti factor? Well, the source equipment fills up those equipment racks, and it will all end up looking neat and tidy.

Over the years there have been many changes in what has been regarded as the norm or an industry standard for the source equipment needed. If you go back far enough you will get to vinyl disks, or were they Bakelite? Then, with the advent of magnetic tape, came the tape recorder revolution. We have steadily worked our way through this age, with things like cassette tapes and DAT tapes, until today we are happily into the digital age, with things such as CDs mini discs, even hard disc recorders. Let me promote the selection of the most used, most popular items.

The CD Player: Where pre-recorded music and certainly effects are concerned, the CD player takes some beating. It's relatively cheap to buy and these days they don't go wrong very often, even when they do, replacement with new is often more cost effective than a repair. One of the big plus points is that they can be accurately cued up, but in choosing a CD player, pay a little extra and buy the professional model, that will probably have nice big buttons

A typical CD player.

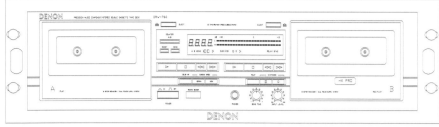

A typical double-cassette player.

with clear legends, whereas the cheaper, domestic machines will have small buttons, fine for home use but not easy to operate in a performance situation. You will notice I have described the CD as a 'player', even though in the last year or so the cost of the CD writer has brought it into almost everyone's budget range and of course this type of unit will play as well as record. My advice would be that if you think you need a CD writer (recorder) then you should have a separate CD player as well. There is a myriad of manufacturers offering similar specifications and, as ever, don't skimp and buy the cheapest, try and stay with a recognised industry standard brand name and, as said, go for the rack-mounting professional model.

The cassette player/recorder: I don't think it matters that much about the combination of the recording and playback functions, and anyway you will find it hard to find a cassette machine that doesn't have both functions. Again, pay the money and buy the rack-mount professional model, if you can afford it, a twin deck machine can be quite useful. Lately, the cassette machine has been rather frowned upon, as being too old fashioned and low-tech to warrant a place in a performance sound system set up. You will know its inherent problems, such as slow tape speed, which generally means lack of sound quality and you just can't cue them up properly. But when the dance festival is taking place and 35 people all turn up with a piece of music, guess what medium it will be recorded on? And in the straight play, what will you use to produce 45 minutes of distant bird songs and general outdoor ambient sound, faintly heard outside the French windows, off stage? Yes, the cassette tape player again, so don't rush to condemn it just yet; it's still got a place in your system and can be very useful.

The mini disc player/recorder: here you have a reasonable choice. Depending on the needs of your venue, you may decide you want two machines anyway, so one is almost bound to be a player/recorder, but you could just buy

A typical mini disk player.

a player for the second machine. The most popular choice is to buy two the same. It records digitally so the quality is good, you can cue it effectively, with instant start up and probably most important of all, the editing and making up of 'show tapes' is a dream. Does anybody want to buy a lot of razor blades and a pile of magnetic tape?

In the smaller budget-conscious sound set up, you may find an acceptable compromise, in using a combined CD and cassette recorder, all packaged into one compact rack-mounting device. It saves a little money and a little space in your equipment rack, but in the really professional workplace, it's not really what you need to use; it's all rather cramped and the operating buttons are small and close together.

So far the equipment (CD, *cassette, mini disk*) has all been specific to the playback or recording of sound, and I have been using words and phrases such as cued up, sound effects, and show tapes, so perhaps a little explanation is needed.

In performance, just as with the changes to the lighting which are now recorded into your memory lighting desk, there is a need to pre-record or at least set up a pre-recorded sound effect.

The advances in computer technology in recent years have provided a vast amount of storage and control of sound sources, within a desktop or laptop computer, and of course it's a simple task to link the output of the computer to the input of your sound mixer, so all your sound effects are just a mouse click away, with all the processing power of whatever system of software your PC is running.

The more traditional (dare I say old fashioned) way of achieving the same result, is by the combined use of equipment like your CD, cassette and mini disc machines. If it's sound effects you are after, the BBC issues a series running to 20 or 30 CDs, covering just about everything imaginable, and if that's not enough there are then one or two specialist suppliers who, if they don't have it already, will make up whatever you want. So just by using the available range of CDs and your CD player, you can solve lots of problems.

By mixing various sounds, some from effects CDs, some perhaps recorded live in your venue, some pre-recorded background sounds, and capturing the end result onto a mini disc, you can fairly simply make up whatever sound you need. For example, played on a backstage loudspeaker you might have a car arriving on a gravel driveway, stopping, doors slamming, footsteps, doorbell ringing, and a gunshot. I'm sure you get the idea, and with the CD and mini disc combination you can record and edit until you have it exactly as required. I called it a 'show tape', a throwback to the days of splicing together a magnetic tape, but today it should more properly be called the 'show disc'.

The critical part of many sound effects is the accuracy of the timing, and this of course has everything to do with the equipment used. In talking about the cassette player, I said you can't cue them up properly, by properly I meant accurately. If you need a gunshot, or even a doorbell to ring, you need it to happen on cue, not a few seconds after you press the play button. By the nature of the machinery involved the cassette player can't give you this degree of accuracy, but a CD player or a mini disc player can, as well as the computer I mentioned.

The name says it all, but with effects processors, if you are still confused, they are mainly concerned with adding to, or modifying a selected sound signal. They can make the sound echo or reverberate, or sound as if it is within a large cavernous space, or by modifying the frequencies within the sound e.g. with a single microphone, the voice can be modified to the point where it sounds more like Donald Duck. It's interesting to note that a very small amount of frequency change, imperceptible to the human ear, can be an aid in that problem area of feedback, indeed there is a range of products called 'feedback eliminators or exterminators' which use this technique. They don't take the feedback problem away, instead what they do is simply to allow a higher level (volume) before the onset of feedback.

Within the effects processor products, there are quite a few to choose from. As with most of the items in this sound source section, you could pay £200 or less for a simple model, or £1000 + for something with all the bells and whistles.

You will remember from the sound mixer section my comments about the auxiliary sends and returns. Well it's this function that permits the use of the effects processor.

8 MICROPHONES

At last, a nice simple topic. Everyone knows what a microphone does? Think again! Yes at its basic level, I think we do all appreciate what a microphone does and I'm not about to shatter your illusions, well not too much, but I'm afraid it's just another minefield of choice, seemingly driven by dozens of manufacturers' desires to make you buy the most recent up-to-date piece of equipment.

At this basic information level, I want to concentrate on just two types of microphone, the dynamic and the condenser. So when people start talking to you about ribbon, or tube/valve, or C-ducer pick-ups, or high impedance figure of eight recording microphones, you will need another more detailed reference book to help you.

The Dynamic Microphone

The dynamic microphone, sometimes called a moving coil microphone, because the *capsule* part that picks up the sound is a magnet that moves within a wire coil. This is all packaged into a relatively small enclosure and, depending on the quality of the microphone, mounted within a shock mount suspension, to keep the handling noise to a minimum.

The dynamic microphone is almost always regarded as a hand-held, or stand-mounted microphone, the user having to be in close proximity to it, and equally regarded almost exclusively as a vocal microphone, although they can be used to pick up instruments as well as the human voice. One of their plus-points is that they are quite rugged and will stand up quite well to the physical abuse they may get during performance. Again, the value for money aspect raises its head. When purchasing a dynamic microphone, anything that costs less than about £50 is, in my view, of poorer quality. You probably need to be spending closer to £100 to get something worthwhile and you could even spend quite a bit more.

The dynamic microphone is the workhorse microphone. It's what everyone knows, and is the shape of a microphone that everyone identifies with.

I need to flag up a pet hate of mine, which I hope you won't find too offensive: namely microphones with on/off switches (apart from radio microphones –

see later). I don't use them, specify them or even sell them; indeed I have been known to refuse to sell such a device to a willing customer, for one very good reason: if you give a performer anything with a switch on it, the first thing they will do is switch it off! There you are at the sound mixer position, with the microphone channel open and no sound coming from your performer, and who gets the blame for the microphone not working? It's bad enough that *you* get the blame, but since you or your venue have spent thousands on providing a mixing desk and sound system equipment, not to mention you sitting there actually operating it all, what is the point of putting yet more obstacles in the way of a trouble free performance? If all you needed was a switch, you could have saved a lot of time and trouble. No, real microphones don't have switches, well not on/off switches anyway. You may see discrete switches on the stem of a real microphone, but these are not on/off switches, they are known as bass cut or bass roll off switches. They are there to provide a quick and easy method of reducing handling noise or reduce feedback, as they remove a small element of frequency pick up coverage from the low end frequencies, making the microphone quieter and less susceptible to feedback.

The Condenser Microphone

If you remember when I was talking about the sound mixer, I talked about phantom power, a low voltage (up to a maximum of 48V DC) power supply emanating from the mixer. Well, these microphones are the reason for this low voltage supply. The microphone works not by a moving coil, as in the dynamic microphone, but by a micro-thin flexible diaphragm placed in very close

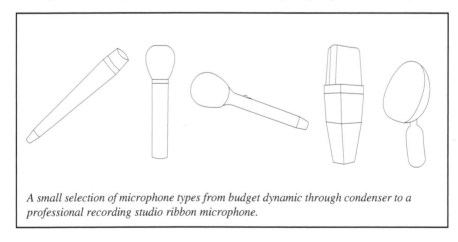

A small selection of microphone types from budget dynamic through condenser to a professional recording studio ribbon microphone.

proximity to a metal plate, where the phantom power voltage provides an electrical charge which, when applied, holds the diaphragm off the metal plate. In very general terms, it's probably fair to say that condenser microphones are better and higher specified than dynamics; they are more sensitive, will in some

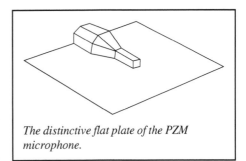

The distinctive flat plate of the PZM microphone.

forms, pick up sounds at a distance away from the microphone, and will perform (pick up) more high frequency sounds than the dynamic. Within the generic family of condenser microphones there are one or two quite special derivatives. The PZM (Pressure Zone Microphone), is sometimes called a 'plate' microphone, in which the actual microphone capsule is contained within an almost flat, small metal plate that is placed on the floor or perhaps on a table, where it collects sound from the surface it is sitting on, sometimes used fixed to 1 or 2 metre squared panels of plywood, or even clear Perspex and placed above the performers. This is very useful in the right environment. Then there is the 'rifle' microphone, the condenser which picks up sound at a distance is almost always a long (300/400mm) tube, often referred to as an interference tube, with perhaps no visible capsule section. It's likely to need a special shock mount microphone clip and maybe a very short microphone stand and will often be used in multiples, 3, 4 or 5 in a line across the front of your stage, providing a pick-up or coverage across the stage and up to 3 or 4 metres away. Again, it's very useful in the right place. There are also smaller versions of the rifle condenser, sometimes only the size of a pencil, which are often seen and used in pairs, on a lectern. Again, in its smaller form the condenser can be used as a high quality hand-held vocal microphone, often physically smaller than the comparable dynamic and of course there are literally dozens of derivatives which have specific characteristics, designed for use with a specific musical instrument.

Within the family or range of condenser microphones, you will come across about four descriptive names: omni, cardioid, hyper-cardioid and figure-of-eight, although the last of these is probably regarded as most used in recording, rather than live performance work.

By way of explanation:

omni – has a pick up characteristic often represented by a circular

Omni-directional pick-up pattern.

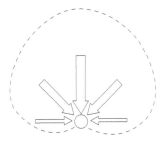

Cardioid pick-up pattern.

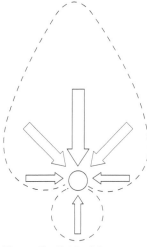

Hyper-Cardioid pick-up pattern.

pattern surrounding the whole microphone, in other words it picks up sound from all around, not specifically in front of it. It is very useful as a microphone picking up sound for transmission into a show relay system (more of this later).

cardioid – has a pick up pattern often represented as an inverted heart shape, with the stem of the microphone at the bottom, the requirement being that most sound is picked up in front of the microphone.

hyper-cardioid – has a pick-up pattern represented by a small circle directly in front of the microphone. Like the cardioid, it only picks up sound from in front, but with a much tighter range, making it ideal for hand held vocals where only the immediate performer's output is needed. It also is less susceptible (but not immune) to feedback.

Your toolbox of microphones should have some of both: dynamic and condenser, although the actual specification of the latter may be a little difficult to determine. If you are unsure, seek advice and remember to include the other important peripheral, namely a selection of microphone stands.

Stating the obvious, but with my now familiar overtones of money buying quality, don't forget the microphone cable that will be needed to connect each microphone into your system. All professional microphones should have a 3 pin XLR connector. It therefore follows that the microphone cable will also use the same connector, so it's really only the specification of the actual cable that can let you down. Use the brand name quality product and don't be surprised if, through use, they need to be replaced every now and then.

I said I wanted to concentrate on just two microphone types, and then I went on about microphones not having switches. Well, I forgot radio microphones, and before you write to tell me, yes I know they have on/off switches! Incidentally, quite a number of the systems available on the market today have some way of making the on/off switch tamper-proof, so hopefully your artiste won't be tempted to fiddle!

Radio Microphones

Radio microphones, here goes. Until quite recently – around three to five years ago – we all used to suffer, and I do mean suffer, with Radio microphones, because for most of us they operated in the VHF (Very High Frequency) waveband and as such were always subject to signal interference and signal drop out. Happily those days are now behind us, because with the advances in technology and cost reductions in electronic components, we can all now afford the far superior UHF (Ultra High Frequency) types. The UHF systems have always been available, but at between £1000 and £3000 each, not many people could afford them. The modern UHF radio microphone is a two-part system. The first part is the transmitter, hand-held or belt-pack, plus a discrete lapel microphone. This system is known as the 'lavalier' (meaning a cord used to suspend something around the neck in French). The second part is the receiver, a small either desktop or rack-mounting unit, which normally sits near to the mixer, maybe within your equipment rack, and of course connects to one channel of the mixing desk. For 2, 3 or maybe 4 radio microphones, you may be able to use the antenna (aerial) that is supplied with the receiver, but for higher multiples, you will almost certainly need a distributed antenna system.

The frequency, or rather the use of a specific frequency used by a radio microphone, is strictly regulated. In the UK, this is done by the Radio Communications Agency, a department of the Home Office, although in order to police the use and allocation of the frequencies, this organisation appoints another company to sort out all the paperwork. Your equipment supplier should be able to give you all the relevant details. Within the regulations laid down by the RCA, there is an allocation for a specific segment of the UHF frequency, which is classed as de-regulated. In effect, this means that anyone has free use of it. By this I mean you don't need a licence to operate your radio microphone, but you still have to buy the equipment! For users who find it necessary to operate outside the de-regulated frequency allocation, maybe because of the high numbers of radio microphone systems in use, e.g. a big West End style musical could use 30 or 40 separate radio microphone channels, then a licence will be required. It's important to note, in this situation, that it's the site that is granted the licence, not the actual equipment, although the equipment being used must conform to the specifications laid down by the RCA for radio microphone equipment. Regulations and licences aside, the modern UHF radio microphone is much more stable and trouble free these days, but there is one thing that you can do to help matters.

Batteries: depending on the manufacturer, your radio microphone transmitter will probably use either AA, AAA, or 9V PP3 type batteries and in reading the manufacturer's information on power consumption, you will see that your radio microphone will run for 8-12 or 15 hours on a set of batteries. Yes, it might, but your new battery may not be as new as you thought. If you happen to have purchased it from a batch of old shelf stock, yes, I know that's very unlikely, but if it's going to happen, it's bound to happen to you! Anyway, you might forget just how many performance hours your microphone has been on for and I guarantee that it will fail during the performance. The only safe way to get around this problem is to use new batteries for every performance. I know it's more expense, but it's another of those seemingly insignificant little things that can affect the successful delivery of your sound system performance.

9
TECHNICAL COMMUNICATIONS AND PAGING EQUIPMENT

Technical Communications

As with all the other technical disciplines involved in the performance arts, the sound operator/s will need to receive cues from stage management. *Basics – A Beginner's Guide to Stage Lighting,* I had quite a lot to say and explain about the stage management function in the technical side of a performance (ref: *Basics – A Beginner's Guide to Stage Lighting,* p65-67), so I won't cover that again here, but what is relevant is that it calls for another dedicated set of equipment needed to deliver the technical talk, known as Technical Communications.

The first thing to understand is that the equipment involved is totally separate from the performance related equipment. There are no shared components or wiring, the only link is that some of the equipment may get installed into one of the much vaunted equipment racks and that some of the connections' positions may appear within the facility panels discussed in chapter 5 of this book.

The hub of the technical communications system is called a 'master' or 'base' station; this is simply a small dedicated amplifier that will run either two or three 'rings' or separate circuits. Each ring or circuit may be run alongside another, having outlet termination boxes in the same locations, but with an 'A' and 'B' ring indicated. They may also be run totally separately from different parts of the building.

The operator, nominally the stage management person who is cueing the show, will be working in close proximity to the base station, so will be able to select which of the rings are going to receive the cues given. It may be that for instance, lighting and sound are set up on ring 'A', while everyone else is on ring 'B'. There is no particular right and wrong way to do this, it is a matter of personal preference on the part of the stage management team and may, to some degree, be dictated by the layout of the building. It can also change from production to production, as needs arise.

The users of this type of system will each wear a headset, either single or double muff type, which has a small boom microphone attached. This headset connects to a small 'belt pack' which clips onto the user's belt, and a relatively

A single-muff 'comms' headset.

short flexible cable (3-5 metres) connects the belt pack to the nearest 'A' or 'B' ring connection point. The belt pack will have an on/off control switch for the microphone, a volume control for the headset, and a 'call' light and switch, which simply flashes all the other call lights in all the other belt packs connected to the same ring. This relatively simple set-up permits the spoken word flow of information between all technical operators and is regarded as an industry standard requirement for all performance arts venues.

You are probably thinking, fine, I accept the need for the technical communications link, but why can't it use radio signals, like the radio microphones? Well, if you have the budget, it can do. But remember, unlike a radio microphone, this function needs to send and receive, so the costs are double. Anyway, for most technical operators, their workstation is a fixed location, so the mobility of a radio signal system is not that vital. In fact, what is common practice, is to find that just one or two radio set adaptors are used within a fixed wiring set-up, to provide the flexibility needed by people who are mobile but still need to be on the technical communications system.

There are quite a few variations within the technical communications equipment: there are dual circuit belt-packs, so that the wearer can pick up both the 'A' and 'B' ring information, there are loudspeaker outstations, and telephone handsets. The planning of the technical communications system can be quite a complex matter. However, in its simplest form, it can be provided as a temporary system, as long as you can cope with the loose cable all over the place. Just to keep things sensible, the wiring used, indeed even the short link cables, are the same specification as used for the performance microphones, a twin screened signal cable being terminated in a 3 pin XLR connector.

Paging Equipment

This has a number of different names or titles: Dressing Room or Backstage Paging, or Show Relay, or FOH Calls. The system that I'm going to describe covers all of these functions. Let's start with dressing room or backstage paging. It's another totally separate, stand-alone system that has nothing to do with the performance sound system or the technical communications system.

The requirement being to provide a means of making announcements from the stage (stage management prompt desk position) into the dressing rooms and backstage areas, while at the same time providing the transmission of the sound from the stage, into the same dressing rooms and backstage areas – this part being known as the show relay.

If you stop and think about it, you have a conflict of interests here, since the artists in the dressing rooms want to hear the action on stage, but they also need to receive 'calls' when necessary from the stage management team to get them to the side of the stage in good time for their entrance, with all of that information coming out of one loudspeaker in each dressing room. The sound input side is relatively simple, you suspend an omnidirectional microphone above the stage acting area, which feeds via an amplifier, into the dressing room loudspeakers, and then at a side stage position (stage management prompt desk), another microphone provides the 'call' facility, via the same amplifier, feeding into the dressing room loudspeakers. The problem is that the important calls to get the artist down on stage in good time can get lost in with the show relay sound. The cure to this is a small piece of circuitry called 'volume restoration'. This cuts in when the calls microphone is activated, thus reducing or totally removing the show relay signal, so that the call can be heard. When the call has finished, the volume is restored, putting the show relay sound back in place.

The loudspeakers in the dressing rooms can sometimes be a cause for concern, as there will usually be some good reason why the show relay sound is not wanted, so you fit a simple volume control to enable the sound to be turned down or off; problem solved, but then the important calls can't be heard! This problem is solved by the use of the volume restoration circuitry that I mentioned, in fact it's a small PCB (Printed Circuit Board) that fits within the loudspeaker and allows the calls information to bypass the volume control, so the calls can be heard, even if the user has turned off the show relay sound. This is quite a small detail, but it makes the dressing room paging system much more user-friendly. There is a small price to pay for this feature, since the volume restoration PCB is an extra cost, along with the volume control and a small upgrade in the wiring needed to make it all work. You could or course leave it out, including the volume control, but then you will probably find out that your performers are all budding technicians, who produce screwdrivers out of their make up bags and disconnect the loudspeaker altogether!

Then we need to cater for those FOH Calls into the bars, foyer, toilets and other areas where the public will gather. It's not a regular requirement to provide a show relay sound source to the FOH areas, but it is normally a stage management function to make announcements into those public areas, such as: "Ladies and gentlemen, tonight's performance will commence in five minutes, please take your seats", etc. So, here we have another use for the microphone at the side stage position (within the stage management prompt desk), except that it now has to talk to another set of loudspeakers, so it needs a selection switch and the system will need an additional amplifier. Indeed it may be found that either within the backstage area or in the FOH, there is a requirement to split the sound into smaller or specifically different areas. Each time this is a requirement, it adds an amplifier to the system and another selection switch to the microphone on stage, each being known as a 'zone'. Fortunately, many manufacturers, in recognising this requirement, have multi-zone systems available, so apart from the unexpected costs involved, we have the technology available to solve the problem.

All of these zones (minimum two) and amplifiers associated with them plus, in all likelihood, a zone selection switcher, provide another couple of units to fit into those equipment racks. You see? I said they were useful, and if they weren't there, just where would you put all your newly acquired paging equipment?

I have described both the technical communications and the paging system as being separate and dedicated systems separate from the main performance sound system and also from each other. I always try very hard to argue the case for this, but there may be an exception. In a small venue set up, where there is no FOH calls requirement and only a very small number of dressing rooms or backstage areas, it may be possible to use the technical communications equipment, specifically with the use of the paging loudspeaker unit that I mentioned, to fulfil both roles. Since most master base station units will have provision for an external microphone to be connected, thus providing the show relay function, then it's just a case of dedicating one ring or circuit to the dressing rooms and the other to the technical areas. I'm not a big fan of this method of use, but I concede that in certain venues, it makes economic sense.

10 OTHER SOUND 'THINGS'

Induction Loops Versus Infrared Transmission

Hearing aid systems are a rather thorny issue, but before I take sides, let's just be clear about what we are dealing with. The induction loop system has for years been regarded as the standard (and not just in performing arts) way of providing an amplified broadcast sound signal into an area to be received by people wearing hearing aid devices, or by wearing a dedicated headset, tuned to pick up the broadcast signal. For hearing aid wearers, there is a multi-position switch on the hearing aid, with on/off and 'T' positions. When switched to the 'T' position, the hearing aid picks up the broadcast signal. The actual induction loop equipment is very simple, it consists of a microphone to pick up the sounds from the performance area, an amplifier and an aerial wire, which surrounds the seated area. This is often a single cable or flat ribbon type cable, laid under the floor or carpet, or hidden behind the decoration or wall covering of the venue.

The infrared transmission system is the modern day, hi-tech method of providing the same function for the aurally impaired, while offering more facilities and doing so to a much higher, better hearing standard. As with the induction loop system, it starts off with a microphone to pick up the sounds from the stage acting area, which is then fed into a modulator – a sort of infrared amplifier. The signal that this generates is fed to one or more infrared radiator panels, which are fixed with a clear line of sight to produce an infrared coverage into the seated area.

At this point, the system differs from the induction loop system, because of the devices that are used by the public in order to receive the infrared signal, which contains the sound signal they need. There are two main types of device used.

The first is for users who already wear a hearing-aid device. It is a small receiver, about the size of a small mobile phone, which has a lanyard, allowing it to be worn around the neck. This serves two functions: it places the receiver at the upper chest area, so with the user looking at the acting area, they will also be looking at the infrared radiator, being strategically placed to cover the seated audience. The second use of the lanyard is to act as an individual, personal induction loop aerial, enabling the user to switch their hearing device to the 'T' position and thus receive the signal, as they would do if using the induction loop system,

The second user-worn device is the same receiver, but instead of a lanyard, this has two flexible earpieces, a little like a doctor's stethoscope, or those headsets you are given on aeroplanes. Incidentally, the actual earpieces are changed after each use, to keep it all hygienic. This is the type of device used by people who don't wear a hearing device, but need some help with hearing the performance.

So what's the problem? Why did I say it was a thorny issue? Well, in these enlightened times we have various pressure groups to fight the corner of the minority groups in our society, one such has been the disability lobby. Now please don't get me wrong here, I'm with these people all the way. The work of such groups have brought about much needed ease of access and many other benefits to the disabled, but when it comes to the issues of induction loop or infrared, there seems to be a move against the infrared systems, because they are seen to highlight the disability, by requiring the users to wear a visible device, whereas with the induction loop system, it's just a matter of changing the switch position on an existing, almost invisible hearing aid. I offer two points for consideration. Firstly, in an induction loop system, if a potential user does not have a hearing aid device, they will need to wear a headset. Does this not also flag up the disability? Secondly, the clarity and overall better performance of the infrared system is so much better than that provided by the induction loop, that it is depriving those affected from the best possible help.

As if that were not a reasonable argument, there are other important factors about the infrared system, which are not easy to replicate with the induction loop system. The broadcast signal used in the induction loop system is a single set frequency. Obviously, all hearing-aid devices that use the 'T' position facility have the same in-built set frequency. The infrared system can output a stereo A & B signal, so you could have a true stereo signal, for a better quality of sound, but that's not how this function is best used. As well as the obvious benefits to the hard-of-hearing, there has been much recent use of 'blind describing' within performance venues. This consists of a describer – someone seated, usually in a soundproofed room or technical area – giving commentary on the actions on stage, so one of the available channels could be used to provide this blind describing service, while the other remains for use by the aurally impaired. And that's not the end of it. Having dual channel signals can also provide a translation service, and all working from the same infrared system, although this system would be slightly more expensive, as the user-worn receivers cost a little more in the dual channel/stereo format.

As ever, there are good points and drawbacks with each system. The induction loop is simple and relatively cheap to buy, but it has its limitations and in some buildings the application of the loop aerial can be a mechanical problem. The infrared system is typically three times the cost, but the quality is far better and it can do so much more. One note of caution: it can't be used in any sort of outdoor venue, since natural light, which contains the infrared spectrum, will downgrade the signal and make it unusable. The user-worn receivers have to be recharged after each use, as they work with small rechargeable cell batteries, and the whole issue of managing their distribution and re-collection from the public, is something not to be overlooked.

You may well find that grant aid is available, where you are providing a hearing system (of either type) into a venue, where there was not one installed previously. The choice is really up to you, but my preference is strongly in favour of the infrared system.

Fire Alarm Interfaces

Fire Alarm interfaces and Voice Evacuation systems are two things that sound as if they should be related, but they are not at all.

For the Fire Alarm interface you will need to seek guidance from your local authority, probably the department that issues the performance licence for your venue, and maybe the local fire authority. They may have a requirement that your performance sound system shuts down in the event of fire alarm activation, the reason being that without sound the performance would have to stop, and the evacuation of the audience would then follow. You may also find something similar being a requirement for the performance lighting system.

If you have adopted one of the power distribution units, mentioned in chapter 4, then it's a relatively simple task to connect this to your fire alarm panel, whereby, when the panel activates, the performance sound system will shut down.

Voice Evacuation

Unlike the previous fire alarm link, Voice Evacuation systems are a completely different proposition. Yes, yet another completely stand alone system is installed within your building. It will probably replicate the positions covered by your backstage and FOH paging system, but there can be no cross-over replication, because the equipment, especially the wiring associated with it, will be specified and installed to a fire resistant standard, not used or required by the paging system. On the activation of the fire alarm, the VA system will output a pre-recorded message, advising people to leave the building.

Because of the fire proof ratings called for in VA systems, you will find that they are an expensive part of your planning, but if it is a requirement you won't be allowed to leave it out, or downgrade it to make it cheaper.

Noise Limiters

Again, it may seem that this has links with some of the other things in this section, but no, it's yet another stand-alone piece of kit. I have included a brief description here, even though it's not truly a piece of sound equipment, but many people perceive that it is, so here goes.

There are two different types and the first is quite simple. It's a small unit that sits inside one of your equipment racks, the sound output signal from the mixer being fed into it, where the device will have a pre-set maximum limit (set by you). When this is reached or exceeded, you will probably get a warning light on the unit, and if the level is not reduced within a prescribed time, the unit will automatically either reduce the level or cut it altogether.

The second type of unit does more or less the same thing, but here it relies on a microphone picking up the ambient sound level within your auditorium. This will provide a flashing light warning, that if the sound level is not reduced, the unit will activate. But its activation will trip a relay device that will disconnect the mains power supply. This is often used on ring main power circuits (13 Amp sockets in your hall) and is designed and intended to combat the mobile disco user, who comes into your hall for perhaps just one night, and refuses to keep their sound equipment to a sensible level.

11 CONCLUSIONS

As users of a performance sound system, you will come from a wide knowledge and experience base, so I have no way of knowing just how helpful, or not, these few pages have been to you. I hope that looking at the overall picture and taking on my comments about how the overall result can and will be affected by so many seemingly insignificant things, like the grade of loudspeaker cable used, or the need for a clean power supply. You can see now just how difficult it is, when you are asked to dip into an existing system of equipment, in an effort to produce a magic solution to a particular problem. It's just not that easy.

A large part of the problem, especially with an existing system, but it also crops up in new-build situations, is the firm and often intransigent views and beliefs held by those people who are tasked with putting a system together, who simply don't have the field experience to make the right decisions. Their thinking is often based on any number of flawed ideas. It maybe a reworking of a previous system, which didn't get the job done either, or a slavish following of a particular brand or type of equipment, which really isn't suited to the job in hand, or, worst of all, someone has set a budget, so that's the level of spend that will provide you with your sound system, with absolutely no thought or reference to the room acoustic or the end user requirements.

I am always very cautious when people set budgets for performance sound systems, where they are following some guidelines for a room budget, within a new build. The planners and cost consultants involved in these sorts of projects have hardly ever experienced the actual requirements of a performance space, so how can they have any meaningful input into the costing of it?

You must be thoroughly fed up by now with my continued references to 'weakest links' and 'spending money'. Well, good. If nothing else, I must have got those two points over. Of course it's all relative to your own personal viewpoint. You may consider that spending £1500 on one pair of loudspeakers, when you had expected to spend £2000 for the whole sound system, is way above both your budget and your expectations, and perhaps you are happy to risk one or two downgrades in the overall specification, due to the budget. Or maybe you feel that I am being over cautious, in flagging up a weak point at almost every turn. You could be right, and if it works for you that's great. I don't want to be seen to be advocating a belts-and-braces approach to all of this, but my comments are born of many years of watching, listening, specifying, advising, and learning about what is contained in this book.

I don't claim to have all the answers, and this book really only scratches the surface of the subject. As I said right at the beginning, a little information can perhaps be a dangerous thing, and this title is only intended to give snapshot information, in the most *basic* form. I hope you have found some little part of it helpful, even if only to delve deeper into the subject, or perhaps to decide that painting the set and scenery would be an easier life.

GLOSSARY

This list is by no means comprehensive; it is intended only to give a quick reference to those names and phrases which cause most confusion to the beginner.

Acoustic: (natural acoustic) Pertaining to sound/hearing, in the 'natural' classification; sound which is not amplified, 'natural acoustic' of a room or space.

Amplifier: Normally (but not always) a stereo (two channel) device, to amplify a sound signal, used after the output of the sound mixer, the output of the amplifier connects to the loudspeakers

Balanced/ Unbalanced: The format of wiring used to connect a sound signal (microphone or other source) to the sound mixer, see text for details, page 42

Cardioid: Relating to the polar pattern (pick up) of condenser microphones, see text for details, page 60

Cassette Player/ Recorder: The basic item of equipment, with which to record and playback sound, regarded as inferior to most other formats, because of its small tape and slow speed.

CD Player: Compact disc player, also available in a recording version, the modern format used to store and replay recorded sounds.

Compression Driver: One of the loudspeaker devices used within a loudspeaker enclosure, see text for details, page 21

Condenser Microphone: Requires a small DC voltage with which to operate, available in a number of different configurations, see text for details, page 58

Dispersion: Relating to the coverage or angle of sound distributed from a loudspeaker, see text for details, page 24

Decibel: One of the measurements of a sound signal, see text for details, page 19

DSP: Digital signal processor, a modern device to enable the modification of sound signals, see text for details, page

Dynamic: Relating to microphones, the general use type, see text for details, page 57

Equipment Rack: A metal cabinet (rack) with an open front and back, fitted with mounting strips and captive nuts, into which 'rack mounting' equipment can be fitted, see text for details, page 35

Facility Panel: A combination of various outlets and connector types, sited around the performance space, see text for details, page 40

Feedback: High pitched whistling sound, caused by a microphone being used at a high gain level, see text for details, page 46

Fire Alarm Interface: A requirement or device which will disable the sound system upon the activation of a building fire alarm, see text for details, page 69

Flat: The descriptive condition of sound without reverberation, see text for details, page 13

Frequency: One of the descriptions used in detailing sound signals, see text for details, page 19

Graphic Equaliser: Equipment which modifies individual frequencies within a sound signal, see text for details, page 33

GPO Patch: A rack mounted panel or multiple Jack sockets, used to terminated and route sound signals, see text for details, page 39

Headroom: Function of planning and designing to ensure that equipment and systems are not over-stressed, see text for details, page 29

Horn: Used in conjunction with a compression driver, as part of a loudspeaker, see text for details, page 21

Hypercardioid: Relating to the polar pattern (pick up) of condenser microphones, see text for details, page 60

Hz (Hertz): Description of the frequency of a sound signal, see text for details, page 19

Intelligibility: Critically the level of intelligibility found within the sound produced, see text for details, page 14

Induction loop:	A system normally associated with the hearing impaired, by which a broadcast signal is provided within the auditorium, for use by hearing aid wearers, page 67
Infrared Transmission:	A system which uses the infrared spectrum, as the carrier for one or more audio signals, see text for details, page 67
Jack Patch:	As GPO patch, see text for details, page 39
Jack Plug:	One of the industry standard connectors, used in sound equipment, either in mono or stereo format, although there are a number of derivatives, the 1¼" is the type used in professional sound systems, see text for details, page 43
Linear Fader:	Within the sound mixer, a flat strip fader, rather than a rotary type, making critical settings easier for the operator.
Loudspeaker:	Various types, sizes and options, see text for details, page 21
Microphones:	See various types: Omnidirectional, Cardioid, Hypercardioid, see text for details, page 57
Mini Disc:	Recording and playback equipment, using a digital format to store and replay recorded sounds, see text for details, page 54
Mixer:	Equipment used to combine, modify and distribute sound signals, see text for details, page 47
NL4:	Connector dedicated for use in the connection of loudspeakers and loudspeaker wiring, see text for details, page 30
Noise Limiter:	A device for limiting the sound level, see text for details, page 70
Normalising:	A method of wiring or signal routing, in conjunction with GPO Jack patch panels, see text for details, page 39
Omnidirectional:	Relating to the polar pattern (pick up) of condenser microphones, see text for details, page 59

Paging Equipment Systems:	Dedicated equipment, providing voice paging and show relay, outside of the auditorium, see text for details, page 64
Phantom Power:	A small DC voltage (between 9 > 48v) required to operate condenser microphones, see text for details, page 58
Potentiometer:	A rotary control, found on sound mixing desks and other equipment. Often abbrviated to 'pot'.
RCA:	Radio Communications Agency, the national organisation which regulates the use of radio frequencies, for information contact JFMG at (020) 7261 3797 see text for details, page 61
Reflections:	Usually relating to reverberation, see text for details, page 16
Reverberations:	Caused by the shape and construction of a building, see text for details, page 13
Signal/Clip Limiter	Circuitry within a power amplifier, or a dedicated external device, which controls and limits the range of a sound signal, normally at the upper or lower extremities.
Soft Start Power Up:	Circuitry within a power amplifier, or other equipment, which turns on the equipmet in sequential order, preventing damage to system equipment from power or signal surges.
Source Equipment:	Any equipment that produces or generates sound.
SPL (Sound Pressure Levels):	The level or volume of sound expressed in decibels (dBs), see text for details, page 24
Stereo:	A sound signal comprising of a Left and Right component.
Technical Communications (Talk Back):	A dedicated system for providing speech links between technical operators, see text for details, page 63
Tweeter:	One of the loudspeaker devices used within a loudspeaker enclosure, see text for details, page 21
Voice Evacuation System:	A dedicated system (including specialist wiring) which provides a voice massage, broadcast into the public areas of a venue, see text for details, page 69

Woofer: Sometimes referred to as a driver, one of the loudspeaker devices used within a loudspeaker enclosure, see text for details, page 21

XLR: The industry standard sound signal connector, in performance sound the 3 pin connector is used. NB. other performance related technical equipment may use the XLR connector in one of its other pin configurations (4, 5, 6 or 7 pin types).

ENTERTAINMENT TECHNOLOGY PRESS

FREE SUBSCRIPTION SERVICE

Keeping Up To Date with

Basics
A Beginner's Guide to Stage Sound

Entertainment Technology titles are continually up-dated, and all major changes and additions are listed in date order in the relevant dedicated area of the publisher's website. Simply go to the front page of www.etnow.com and click on the BOOKS button. From there you can locate the title and be connected through to the latest information and services related to the publication.

The author of the title welcomes comments and suggestions about the book and can be contacted by email at: basics@etnow.com

Titles Published by Entertainment Technology Press

ABC of Theatre Jargon *Francis Reid* **£9.95**
This glossary of theatrical terminology explains the common words and phrases that are used in normal conversation between actors, directors, designers, technicians and managers.

Aluminium Structures in the Entertainment Industry *Peter Hind* **£24.95**
Aluminium Structures in the Entertainment Industry aims to educate the reader in all aspects of the design and safe usage of temporary and permanent aluminium structures specific to the entertainment industry – such as roof structures, PA towers, temporary staging, etc.

Basics - A Beginner's Guide to Stage Lighting *Peter Coleman* **£9.95**
This title does what it says: it introduces newcomers to the world of stage lighting. It will not teach the reader the art of lighting design, but will teach beginners much about the 'nuts and bolts' of stage lighting.

The Exeter Theatre Fire *David Anderson* **£24.95**
This title is a fascinating insight into the events that led up to the disaster at the Theatre Royal, Exeter, on the night of September 5th 1887. The book details what went wrong, and the lessons that were learned from the event.

Health and Safety Aspects in the Live Music Industry *Chris Kemp, Iain Hill* **£30.00**
This title includes chapters on various safety aspects of live event production and is written by specialists in their particular areas of expertise.

Hearing the Light *Francis Reid* **£24.95**
This highly enjoyable memoir delves deeply into the theatricality of the industry. The author's almost fanatical interest in opera, his formative period as lighting designer at Glyndebourne and his experiences as a theatre administrator, writer and teacher make for a broad and unique background.

Focus on Lighting Technology *Richard Cadena* **£17.95**
This concise work unravels the mechanics behind modern performance lighting and appeals to designers and technicians alike. Packed with clear, easy-to-read diagrams, the book provides excellent explanations behind the technology of performance lighting.

An Introduction to Rigging in the Entertainment Industry *Chris Higgs* **£24.95**
This book is a practical guide to rigging techniques and practices and also thoroughly covers safety issues and discusses the implications of working within recommended guidelines and regulations.

Lighting for Roméo and Juliette *John Offord* **£26.95**
John Offord describes the making of the production from the lighting designer's viewpoint - taking the story through from the point where director Jürgen Flimm made his decision not to use scenery or sets and simply employ the expertise of Patrick Woodroffe.

Lighting Systems for TV Studios *Nick Mobsby* **£35.00**
Lighting Systems for TV Studios is the first book written specifically on the subject and is set to become the 'standard' resource work for the sector as it covers all elements of system design – rigging, ventilation, electrical as well as the more obvious controls, dimmers and luminaires.

Lighting Techniques for Theatre-in-the-Round *Jackie Staines,* **£24.95**
Lighting Techniques for Theatre-in-the-Round is a unique reference source for those working